BEARING WITNESS

The EFPP Book Series

BEARING WITNESS
Psychoanalytic work with people traumatized by torture and state violence

Editors

*Andrés Gautier and
Anna Sabatini Scalmati*

Routledge
Taylor & Francis Group

LONDON AND NEW YORK

First published 2010 by Karnac Books Ltd.

Published 2018 by Routledge
2 Park Square, Milton Park, Abingdon, Oxon OX14 4RN
711 Third Avenue, New York, NY 10017, USA

Routledge is an imprint of the Taylor & Francis Group, an informa business

British Library Cataloguing in Publication Data

A C.I.P. for this book is available from the British Library

ISBN-13: 978-1-85575-796-7 (pbk)

Typeset by Vikatan Publishing Solutions (P) Ltd., Chennai, India

CONTENTS

v

ABOUT THE EDITORS AND CONTRIBUTORS

Silvia Amati Sas (Italy) studied medicine in Buenos Aires and specialized in child psychiatry at the University of Geneva, Switzerland. She is an AFT member of the Swiss Society of Psychoanalysis and ordinary member of the Italian Psychoanalytic Society. She has published several papers on social traumatic violence, a number of which have been published in English, including: *Thoughts on Torture* (Free Association, 1988); *Ethics, Shame and Countertransference* (Psychoanalytic Inquiry, Vol. 12, 570–579, 1992); *Ambiguity as the Route to Shame* (The International Journal of Psychoanalysis, Vol. 73, 329–334, 1992) and *Traumatic Social Violence: Challenging our Unconscious Adaptation* (International Forum of Psychoanalysis, Vol. 13, 51–59, 2004).

François Fleury was born in 1947 and is a graduate of the University of Grenoble. He was consulting assistant in psychology for Professor Letizia Comba-Jervis for over 20 years, at the Italian universities of Urbino (1976–1984) and Verona (1985–1999). Since 1983, he has worked as a psychotherapist with migrant populations. Co-founder of the "Appurtenances" association in Lausanne, he has worked there as an ethno-therapist from 1993 to the present day. He has written a number of studies and articles on the problems of mental health related to migration and exile.

Andrés Gautier (Bolivia) is a psychotherapist specializing both in adolescents and adults. He has worked for many years in Switzerland as a psychoanalyst, psychotherapist, and supervisor in both private practice and penitentiary institutions. He is coordinator of the EFPP working group on "Trauma and State Violence". In 2001, together with Emma Bolshia Bravo, he founded the Institute for Therapy and Research on the Sequels of Torture and State Violence (ITEI) in La Paz, Bolivia. He is co-publisher of the interdisciplinary research in Spanish: *La Represión de la Marcha por la Sobrevivencia—sobre las secuelas psico-sociales de la violencia estatal*. In 2004, he published an article in "Psychothérapies" entitled: *Les Anciens Marchent sur La Paz (Bolivie). De l'Usage Pluridisciplinaire du Témoignage dans la Recherche Psychosociale Psychanalytique*, Geneva, Vol. 24, N. 4 pp. 223–235.

Liselotte Grünbaum (Denmark) is a registered MSc psychologist, supervisor, psychotherapist, and child psychotherapist. She is a founder member of the Danish Association of Psychoanalytic Child and Adolescent Psychotherapy, took part in the first training committee, and is still a supervisor and teacher on the training committee. She is in private practice, formerly working at a public child guidance clinic and at the Rehabilitation and Research Centre for Torture Victims in Copenhagen. She is coordinator of research for EFPP, formerly coordinator of the Child and Adolescent Section. Publications available in English include: *Children in torture-surviving families: child psychotherapy within a family-orientated context* (J. Pestalozzi (Ed.), Psychoanalytic Psychotherapy in Institutional Settings, Karnac, 1998); *Psychotherapy with children in refugee families who have survived torture: containment and understanding of repetitive behaviour and play* (Journal of Child Psychotherapy, Vol. 23(3), 1997); *Witches howl on New Year's Eve* (Journal of Child Psychotherapy, Vol. 23(1), 1997); co-author with M. Gammeltoft, *Young Children of Schizophrenic Mothers: Difficulties of Intervention* (American Journal of Orthopsychiatry, Vol. 63(1), 1993).

Katharina Ley (Switzerland) is a psychoanalyst/psychotherapist, sociologist, and author. She works in private practice and in a crisis intervention institution in Bern. From 2001–2004 she worked in a trauma clinic in Johannesburg, South Africa. Her most recent publications include: *Überlebenskünstlerinnen. Frauen in Südafrika* (2004); *Versöhnung mit den Eltern. Wege zur inneren Freiheit* (2005); *Komm zu dir, dann geht es weiter. Es ist nie zu spät, sich selbst zu lieben* (2007), and *Geschwisterbande— Liebe, Hass und Solidarität* (Neuauflage, 2007).

Shadman Mahmoud-Shwana (Iraq) was born in 1965 in Kurdistan near Sulaymaniyah, where he completed primary and secondary school and worked in his father's bookshop. In 1983, he left for Baghdad to study pedagogy and English literature and he taught English language. In 1991, he started work as an interpreter/translator for the United Nations and later became a field officer for the organization. In exile since 1996, he has continued working as an interpreter/translator at the same time as studying political science at the University of Lausanne.

Gabriela Mann (Israel) is a training analyst and founder member of the Tel Aviv Institute of Contemporary Psychoanalysis. She teaches and supervises on the Post Graduate Program in Psychotherapy, Tel Aviv University School of Medicine, and is a clinical supervisor at Natal, The Israel Trauma Center for Victims of Terror and War. Dr Mann has also been an active member of Mental Health Professionals for Peace, an organization of mental health professionals concerned with the influence of war on Israelis and Palestinians. She has published several papers about transformation, including: *Transformational, Conservative and Terminal Objects: The Application of Bollas's Concepts to Practice* (in: J. Scalia (Ed.), The Vitality of Objects: Exploring the Work of Christopher Bollas, Continuum International Press, London and Western Univ. Press, USA, 2002); and *Emotional Blindness and its Transformation* (Psychoanalytic Review, *94(2)*, April 2007).

Mary Raphaely (UK) is a group analytic psychotherapist working in London at the Medical Foundation for the Care of Victims of Torture, with a particular interest in societal and cultural contexts in therapy. She has previously worked in prisons with violent offenders and is interested in issues of marginality and exclusion. In addition to working with nature as a metaphor combined with psychotherapy, she conducts more conventional single-sex and mixed groups in French, raising many questions about the implications of language in psychotherapy. In her role as coordinator of the Natural Growth Project, she works with plants and the seasons and believes that nature itself is the language of the soul.

Alejandro Reyes (UK) is a former paediatrician who has practised in Chile, Algeria, and the UK. He trained as a psychoanalytical psychotherapist in Britain and is presently a full member of the Lincoln Centre of Psychotherapy. He has extensive experience in psychoanalytical work with therapeutic organizations and was, until recently, therapeutic consultant to the Mulberry Bush School for emotionally disturbed children.

Paulina Reyes (UK) has worked as a consultant child and adolescent psychotherapist for the Gender Identity Development Service at the Tavistock and Portman NHS Trust. She has extensive experience of psychoanalytical psychotherapy with children and young people with gender identity difficulties. She is currently in private practice.

Paulina and Alejandro Reyes are exiles from the Chilean military coup, now living in London. They had their first therapeutic experiences with exiles and extreme trauma as members of the Latin American Health Professionals, work which they then continued for many years within the NHS, also providing supervision and consultation to refugee organizations. They have both applied the theories of Matte Blanco to their work on trauma and presented and published papers on this subject.

Anna Sabatini Scalmati (Italy) is a psychoanalytical psychotherapist, training and supervising member of the Italian Association of Psychoanalytical Psychotherapy for Children (AIPPI), and member of the Italian Association of Psychoanalytic Psychotherapy for Adults (SIPP). She works through private clinical consultation with both adult and child patients and has a particular scientific interest in the study of primary mental development. She holds psychotherapy sessions with political refugees who are victims of torture or who have survived mass killings. She lives and works in Rome and is author of several articles, including: *Memorie congelate memorie evitate: a proposito della relazione terapeutica con le vittime di torture; Psicoterapia con sopravvissuti a torture, stupri e stragi di massa; "Extracomunitari" e rifugiati politici; Drammi culturali e traumi psichici;* and *La cultura psicoanalitica e il problema guerra, Trauma originario e trauma esterno.*

Monica Lanyado and Didier Houzel

Despite its harrowing subject matter, this is an inspirational book. Based on their work in the ongoing EFPP workshop on psychoanalytic work with the victims of torture and state violence, Andrés Gautier and Anna Sabatini Scalmati have brought together a remarkable group of papers.

The contributors to this volume apply their psychoanalytic training in many different ways to help their child, adolescent, and adult patients, vividly illustrating the flexibility of psychoanalytic techniques that can be developed to help people who have suffered in the most extreme ways. The contributors are working all over the world: Denmark, UK, South America, Israel, France, South Africa, and Italy, coming together to discuss the profound difficulties of their work in the EFPP workshop, gaining support from each other in the process.

Some of the patients are being seen in conventional psychoanalytic settings; intensive open-ended work, but with very special therapeutic needs resulting from the severity of the trauma requiring some adaptations of boundaries in order to sustain the treatment. Others are being seen initially in the practical surroundings of a therapeutic garden before they can begin to bear to approach their terrible trauma through more usual verbal approaches. Psychoanalytic understanding is the key unifying factor, enabling these dedicated clinicians to sustain this very distressing and disturbing work.

Ethical and philosophical questions which are at the core of human conflict are repeatedly raised in these chapters. The reader will be moved, stimulated and richly rewarded by "bearing witness" to the wisdom and humanity in this book.

Monica Lanyado and Didier Houzel

FOREWORD

René Kaës

Under the skilful editorship of Andrés Gautier and Anna Sabatini Scalmati, this book asks both psychoanalysts and politicians a question that goes right to the heart of their "impossible professions". It is a question that lies at the nodal point where two disasters come together; one which wrecks a legally constituted state apparatus and the other which befalls certain individuals who are faced with having to incorporate in their minds, a traumatic irruption originating in a different dimension from that of intra-psychic determinism: the political sphere.

The violence, torture, and assassination to which the state has recourse in order to sustain both its power and the vested interests that it serves, interpellate politicians in terms of their very function and legitimacy. The function of politicians when faced with paranoid or perverse excesses into which the totalitarian state settles, and during which the legally constituted state loses all legitimacy, is to restore the capacity of institutions to guarantee respect for human rights. By doing this, they ensure that citizens can resist such violence in both thought and action so as to safeguard their physical and mental integrity. The borderline case that confronts politicians when the state-run apparatus vitiates its legitimacy is whether to have recourse to violence in order to combat violence. That is, in all probability, a significant feature of their impossible profession.

But after torture, disappearances, and genocide, another question arises, even when the law-abiding nature of the state has been restored. Paul Parin was one of the first to realize this when, in 1983, he argued that the exercise of power and social mourning are incompatible because they raise the question of the responsibility of the state apparatus (Parin, 1983). That analysis has recently been re-examined from a different perspective by J.-C. Metraux (2004); after any kind of mass catastrophe, survival demands that everything should focus on the present and on the primacy of the group over the individual. Sacrificial mechanisms lead to a suspension of the mourning process and perhaps even to its denial, as if a shared depressive phase represents a risk for those in power; that of being held accountable for the violence that they may or may not have directly instigated.[1] According to Parin, the powers-that-be know the potential force of the solidarity and commitment that shared mourning implies. I would add that granting amnesty to those in authority serves the interests of amnesia, the so-called prerequisite for the situation to get back to "normal".

In such circumstances, the forgetting that is necessary for life to continue is impossible. Against the emergence of truth required for the mourning process and the reconstruction of memory, collective denial and perverse alliances encourage, with the support of the state even though it may be law-abiding in character, all sorts of revisionist denials. The original disaster, about the origins and consequences of which no thinking was allowed, generates a further catastrophe; the state imposes an encapsulation both of the violence to which people had been subjected and of any trace that remains of it in each person's mind. This reduplication of archaic violence shuts the door on any process of representation that could afford some sense of the catastrophe. The violence is indeed archaic, because it affects the common foundations of mind and society; it dismantles them.

Psychoanalysts are also faced with possible deadlock in their function. The effects of state-engineered violence, torture, assassination, public denial, and the archaic violence embedded in these situations

---

[1] A. Gautier, however, points out that these sacrificial mechanisms do at least give some scope for acknowledgement of transgression; unlike complete silence, they make it "visible" (personal communication).

bring psychoanalysts face-to-face with the frontier between reality and fantasy in the very experience of trauma that results from them. How are we to think in a psychoanalytic manner about psychological problems that have their roots in what Silvia Amati Sas, in Chapter One of this book, calls social violence?

It is not only a matter of thinking about this domain; we must also think about how the psychoanalyst behaves in such a context. Several of our Latin American colleagues, including Janine Puget and Maren and Marcelo Viñar (1988), have emphasized the fact that it would be too simplistic to consider the experience of torture as solely belonging to the category of physical and psychological violence and aggression. These are no more than the means and instruments of a well thought-out and smooth-running system, the aim of which is to destroy the victims' beliefs and to divest them, as individual persons, of all relationships with themselves, with their ideals, and with their memory. Thus deprived of everything that testifies to their belonging to the human species, they are no longer considered to be human beings. Our fellow psychoanalysts have argued cogently and energetically that the trauma which results from these social catastrophes cannot be imputed to purely psychological factors in line with the model Freud envisaged, based on the theory of fantasy; if that were to be the case, victims would once again be robbed of their historical and real relationship to the actual traumatic event. The only way of doing away with that would be to go along with denial of the trauma produced by state-organized violence. The victim and the psychoanalyst who listens to his or her narrative, must replace the traumatic experience within a political, social space and time framework, restoring the context in which the trauma occurred, in an attempt to make it meaningful both for the victim's personal history and for history itself.

In their discussion of torture, the contributors to this book write of what its victims cannot put into words and the work that has to be done with them to that end. Working with a victim's account of a traumatic experience goes much further than any debriefing technique would have us believe. Above all, victims need someone to listen carefully to what they have to say; that person will be the first to offer a refuge for the pain of those who have no internal "shelter" of their own.

The authors go on to discuss the kind of mental processing that can free victims from their unspeakable trauma, a trauma that has no framework in time or words with which to express it. Grünbaum's chapter on nightmares as means of approaching the unconscious psychic reality that was so terribly disrupted, is consistent with recent studies, for example that of Godard (2003), on working with the dreams of people traumatized by war or survivors of genocide. There are several points of agreement between these studies and my own work. They highlight the importance of representations upon which a whole series of narratives can be based, with their different versions, their reruns, and their deferred impact. Trauma of this nature can be processed only through the polysemy that was condensed when state-engineered violence intruded into the victim's mind.

What happened to each individual victim happened also, under identical conditions and for the same reasons, to others. In my opinion it would be a major limitation of psychoanalytic technique, and in some cases a mistake, were we to restrict our clinical work with victims of state-organized violence to individual treatment, as the traditional psychoanalytic model would have it. I believe that working through the traumatic experience in a group context is not only helpful but also at times absolutely necessary, whenever it is possible to do so. The process of free association in a group, together with the polyphony of its representational modalities, offers the individual the possibility of putting into words phenomena that his or her own capacity for representation and thinking could not, at the time, encompass.

Inter-subjectivity is processed mentally in a group; a multi-vocal narrative is built up by and for several listeners, some of whom have been victims of catastrophe, others witnesses to it, others again untouched by it, which creates the requisite conditions for thinking the unthinkable. This testimony, with its several witnesses, is a prerequisite for any correlative reconstruction of a shared psychological, social, and inter-discursive fabric that belongs to us all. I have suggested that we use the old word remembrance, which exists both in French and in English, to designate the close correlation between polyphonic narrative, reconstructed memory, and inter-subjectivity. Remembrance implies remembering which, in turn, is a reference to the re-membering of people who have been dispersed, blown apart, or dismembered. Remembrance is therefore a process of comemoration.

As Andrés Gautier maintains, it is thanks to this process that a path is opened up from private witness to public testimony. That testimony, to my ears, is the mandate which the dead bequeath to the survivors, the mandate that survivors hand on to subsequent generations.

A time for bearing witness

Anna Sabatini Scalmati and Andrés Gautier

> My good people, don't forget: go and
> tell, my good people, write it down!
>
> —Simon Doubnov

During the last few decades, in mental health institutions and doctors' offices, calls for help have arrived, asking therapists to adapt their traditional theory to the results of events that are wreaking havoc in various parts of the globe. These are chapters of history teeming with horror and death, tidal waves that throw ashore columns of desperate people, castaways from lands and cultures that have been violently torn from them. Refugees from regions oppressed by war, genocide, and social and political brutality; exiles wrenched from their emotional ties, who have watched the collapse of their cultural models, traditions, rites, and the daily rhythms which had regulated their social lives and held collective anxieties at bay.

Many of them have known oppressive incarceration and torture; traumatic violation that engulfs them in a whirlpool of insecurity. They are fugitives who must contend with a wreck that can hardly be decoded, with the failure of community structures in the web of which were woven, for the most part unconsciously, the threads of the intrapsychic, the intersubjective, and the transubjective (Puget, 1995). The social macrocontext has toppled onto their internal world and vice versa. Societal chaos exposes them to states of intense confusion and to a hitherto unknown narcissistic fragility which is aggravated by uprooting them from their lands, and by the inhospitality, if not open hostility, of the countries in which they land.

These are men and women who are marked by a legacy of trauma which, as mental health workers are well aware, goes far beyond the reductive diagnostic category of PTSD. An inheritance of suffering, a sediment, a deposit of death that impairs their mental soundness, blurs their feelings and colonizes their internal world; a disturbing polysemy, a dense contradictoriness of facts, which wipes out speech and reduces their memory capacity.

It is incumbent on mental health workers who witness these dramas to approach the core of these violations and become sensitive containers of memories that can never be translated into thoughts and words and thus alleviated. They must look upon the maelstrom, the terrifying images, and the levels of feeling, at times a dense, hard non-feeling, which these individuals contend with day after day. They must seize shadows of representations which, while not recorded by the conscious imagination, weave unexpected synapses between the "symmetries" of the unconscious (Matte Blanco, 1975).

In the forced migrations and incarcerations this book discusses, human beings become quite simply, meat. The horror and abuse with which these patients have cohabited were only the prologue to what has indelibly marked them: the experience of evil, the presence of the inhuman in the human, and the experience of death in life.

Death did not graze them or touch them in passing; it passed through them and fed them with sham executions, with the agony of a body that goes mad under the merciless lash of unthinkable and uncontainable suffering, with murders and suicides which, against their will, they have had to witness. Again and again they have shaken the hand of death, with its attendant burden of anguish and the grim foreboding of its arrival. Death has gouged areas in them of an undertow, a fatal attraction.

To this legacy, so difficult to decipher, must be added the internalization of abuse. In the name of ethical values and human rights, and with the force of indignation, hatred, and fury, they fought against it but, as a result of the violence they have undergone, the weakening of their bodies, their isolation, the dissolution of emotional ties, and the moral violence of the system, they have at the same time submitted to it. The brute force of those in power has crushed them and made them accomplices of the very evil that struck at them.

The logic of terror, by means of internalizing horror and guilt after corroding areas of their autonomy of thought, and due to the collusion of primitive parts of the psyche, has installed itself in their minds. The internalized external oppressor has deceived and deposed the paternal superego. A tragic internalization which, as it retraces and reactivates other internalizations, has transformed the abuse that was performed externally into internal abuse. Thus the reigning powers have sealed their dominion over the entire person.

But the smothering of affects that has crushed them, the howling that has suffocated their personae, does not stop with their surrender and silence. Affects cannot be repressed. Those affects that do not find an appropriate outlet reappear en bloc in their bodies, or generate significant and debilitating psychic fragility, only to reappear in their children, whose future is marked by them. The emotional working through that a generation does not manage to complete is handed on, like "candles of remembrance" (Wardi, 1990) to the next generation, with the attendant effects on their identity and emotional range.

The presumed dichotomy between the unscathed and the injured creates fault lines that shift onto the former the evil that has injured the latter, leaving the witness the task of restoring a voice to those who are suffering. If this does not take place, if this working through is arrogantly, even triumphantly shunned by their descendants, then persecution looms, and a disturbing spiral comes into being, in which trauma generates other traumas, the past recreating itself in the present where today's anguish is piled upon that of yesterday.

In 1957, Albert Camus, who had witnessed the cataclysm of the Second World War, said in his acceptance speech for his Nobel Prize for Literature, "We writers of the twentieth century [...] must be aware [...] that our only justification [...] is in speaking, to the extent that our abilities permit, for those who are unable to do so."

The pages of this book contain articles by psychotherapists who have been working for years with patients whose lives have been devastated by sudden social and political change. The therapy works towards repairing injured tissue that discharges fearful images and impulses to act; a therapy that from behind the images of destruction and death, picks up the shadows that flicker in the minds of these patients, forming conscious and unconscious visions of violence and cruelty.

These are deposits of "radioactive identifications" (Gampel, 1996), internalizations of violent and destructive aspects of external reality, the presentation of and identification with dramatic experiences which call upon the therapist to differentiate between, on the one hand, the part of destructiveness connected with subjective conflict and existential suffering, and on the other, the part that is linked to the brutality and atrocities of which the patient has been victim and witness. There is the need to decipher the inscriptions carved on the depths of the patient's inner being by the oppressor state, by the brute power of a government which, having bent to its purposes legal, cultural, and religious structures, metasocial bulwarks that support and organize collective life, trigger off, in the victim's internal world, the implosion of metapsychological guarantees (Kaës, 2005).

The analyst must help the patient to overcome the resistance that makes his own history alien to him, estranges him from his feelings and dims his understanding, without meanwhile underestimating the difficulties the analyst encounters in interpreting and becoming witness to the wounds, the levels of isolation and of dissolution of the sense of self that are inflicted on one human being by another.

The traumatic scenes discussed in these pages are extreme expressions of historic and political conditions that are casting shadows of acute instability throughout the world. Trauma, the unexpected, and the pathological are so distinctly present in everyday life that P. Reyes and A. Reyes (p. 41) compare, in their article, the concept of trauma and of the traumatic situation with individual and collective feelings of impotence, together with a sensibility that has been repeatedly contaminated by scenes of horror, experiences of turmoil, emotional and cognitive ambiguities, and non-differentiation, which are by now common to us all, since we have become traumatized witnesses of the horrors of this era. Faced with the fading of the exceptionality of trauma, at a cost to each of us, the threshold of "extreme trauma" has risen. Analysts are the ones who must reconsider the whole therapy of trauma: this is the subject these authors deal with. Analysts must, in other words, construct a model of thought that makes it possible to offer appropriate help to those who have personally suffered the scourge of persecution and torture. It is the only way to avoid diluting their tragedy, their

death-like feelings, and their distinctly diminished subjectivity against
the background of an acutely traumatized society so as not to abandon
and ignore them.

Every page of this volume deals with the raised threshold of
trauma. There are articles by analysts who work in Israel, South
Africa, and Bolivia, all countries where the same sort of "terrain of
instability" affects both therapist and patient. The analysts' care and
sensitivity, informed by experiences not altogether unlike those of their
patients, make it difficult if not impossible to exclude the outside world
from the analytic office. It is impossible not to take that world into
account, although, by using a very fine scalpel, the authors attempt to
re-establish the borders between public and private spheres which have
been effaced by the perverse spiral that tangles political happenings
with social relations and individual attitudes.

In these therapies we can observe how analysts flexibly and carefully
adapt their theoretical and technical paradigms to the conditions of
political and economic instability in which they work. We can also
see how the therapist's desire to approach the patient is often in conflict with the fear, whether conscious or unconscious, of being injured
by the violence of his or her own feelings, of coming upon pockets
of emotional ambiguity, and of taking the measure of his or her own
ideological positions. Gabriela Mann writes of the analyst's difficulty in
being open to the patient's motivations and psychic defences, especially
when the patient comes from a different part of the political spectrum.
She talks about the analysis to which she subjects her own ideas and
ideological positions, so that the other person's reasoning neither taints
the empathetic connection between them, nor obstructs the possibility of being receptive to his or her thinking because, in any case, the
patient comes for therapy burdened with considerable anguish and
torment.

Katharina Ley's essay develops along two dimensions. The first is
the social disintegration, violence, and crimes that after 350 years of
apartheid and little more than a decade of independent democracy,
traverse all of South African society and the ancient culture of oral narration: the narrator, the bard who is linked to an old and deeply rooted
cultural tradition which is related to the language of dreams and the
imagination. Historico-political conditioning and socio-cultural paradigms have meanings which must be understood if one is to prepare
oneself to contain and have a dialogue with the agony of traumatized

generations. Cultural traditions and shared imagery can also be drawn upon as the cement of communal feeling.

Andrés Gautier, who in January 2003, as a psychoanalyst and psychotherapist, listened to accounts of the suffering of Bolivian pensioners marching on La Paz, reflects on the value of testimony. "When [the patient] begins to speak," he writes, "his desire is both to declare the insurmountable aspect of his experience, and to re-establish contact with mankind, with his fellow human being. His testimony thus represents an attempt to re-create some type of link at the point where the break took place." His long experience as a mental health worker has prompted him to ask psychoanalysts, in addition to the work done in their offices, about the painstaking and discreet attention with which they approach the suffering that reverberates throughout the personalities of their patients; to assume the role of witnesses. It is up to them, with their privileged knowledge of the shadows that invade and subdue these patients' minds, and with their awareness that affects cannot be repressed but are passed on to future generations leaving their mark on the future of the species, to expose institutional violence. This is a violence that unleashes a relational barbarity that can silence an entire people and cause profound isolation, depression, panic, and renewed violence in subsequent generations.

The articles by psychotherapists working in Europe show us how cultural and economic discrepancies, language comprehension problems, differing and mutually unfamiliar religions, and transubjective references, create problems for a working therapeutic alliance with patients who have come from the Southern Hemisphere to prosperous European countries. We read in these articles of their mute suffering, the difficulties that make them withdraw into themselves; of the solicitude, the tiny steps with which the analyst gradually approaches the patient and helps him to mend his torn object relations and repair his affective links, to disentangle his identity from the stamp of "inhumanity", to heal the fracture which has proclaimed him a "subhuman", an enemy to be removed, debased, and robbed of his self-image.

They tell us of violent, sanguinary severance from native lands, of marks imprinted on the implicit memory which, finding no correspondence in the patient's current surroundings, confuse him and extinguish all hope. Hope that is not like the unobtainable beloved, but like a map, with a space for registering self-awareness. Hope as the mobilization of projects, allowing a glimpse of possible change and renewal. Hope as a dimension of the mind that can transcend reality.

Due to some juridico-social hocus-pocus, these citizens of the world are denied the right to live in European territory; they are repeatedly asked to renew their residence permits and to limit themselves, as non-EU citizens, to the edges of society. A survival condition that unquestionably becomes pathological if these people, who are already downtrodden, without faith in their own abilities and in despair, are also denied the possibility of recounting their past. If to their pernicious internal alienation, to the denial of their sufferings you add the facet of not seeing or knowing demonstrated by the host society, you have a defence which, while allowing that society to evade its social responsibilities and avoid the anguish, increases its myopia and incapacity to plan a future of mutually beneficial creative communal life.

The harm done by this silence is very evident to François Fleury, who believes that the narrative link that joins the inhabitants of a land to their mythical progenitors plays an important therapeutic role. Narration represents the first realm where they can stand up to the explicit and implicit levels of non-recognition, the lack of protection, the instability that must be contended with day after day, and the moments of profound disorientation. Narration is the realm for standing up to the vicious circle that would seal their lips, so that the social environment that does not care to know them, does not extinguish their desire to be known, and they themselves do not relegate self-expression to the sphere of psychosomatic symptoms and mental illness. Fleury focuses his essay on the role of speech, on paying attention to individual stories, on a place where the patient is listened to and where he can bring back to life his stories, his narrative links. This presents the potential to restore the right to be heard by the bard within them, who can perhaps help them work through their suffering and allow them to see their connections with the history of their people and the symbols of their culture. It can provide a narrative framework that lets their story make contact with their listeners and vice versa. Re-appropriating speech enables them to work on that attitude of standing at a distance which, throughout human history, has made possible the creation of great epics and myths of heroes who, thanks to their wits, escaped unharmed from encounters with oppression and violence.

A careful and for the most part unspoken dream analysis allowed Liselotte Grünbaum to dent the shell of depression, the lethargy that was undermining her young patient's time, thought, and ability to learn and to become socially integrated. Grünbaum approaches the nightmares and recurring states of terror that punctuate his apathy, seeking to gather from them, not so much and not only the cathartic aspect as regards unbearable psychic material, but the signs, the milestones of significant breaking points, the evidence of the collapse of primary links. She draws near them and from them she takes the first steps towards resuscitating symbolic thought and benumbed object relations. A necessary task if one is to fill the empty spaces in which the traumatic reaction, cut off from the constant flow of unconscious symbolism, continually reproduces itself.

The defence of ambiguity, the regressive flight to primitive states of mind in which one can become a collaborator of violent social systems and intolerable life situations, can become acceptable: these are the central themes of Silvia Amati Sas's essay. Here is an analyst with a very good eye for connections between individual and collective history, as well as for the ambiguous nucleus (Bleger, 1967) that, once deposited in the depths of the mind, in certain social conditions, can trap a person in indistinctness and non-differentiation. Without ever losing sight of the intrapsychic, intersubjective, and transubjective spheres, Amati Sas helps her patient recover the strands of her inner self which had been tangled by the violence and perversity of her gaolers. She assists her in freeing herself from distorted introjections and from the perverse appeal of non-differentiation which had left their mark on her mind.

In the gardens of the Natural Growth Project, with nature as a transitional space, a place for a possible first approach to the wounds of the body and the psyche, Mary Raphaely sows the seed of a possible therapeutic meeting. Here exists a project that combines group and, wherever possible, individual psychotherapy with gardening in the park. From the life of nature, with its rhythms and ways, springs this attempt to draw nearer to the patients' emotional lives, their inner worlds, and the parts of their feelings that are frozen to numbness.

Clinical work with an African adolescent who, in the course of long months of imprisonment and torture, underwent catastrophic affective and sensory acceleration, shows, in the case presented by Anna Sabatini Scalmati, how therapy with these patients, if it is to succeed in reactivating the mental processes of differentiation, ambivalence, and contradiction, must first become the receptacle, the repository of aspects of shame, anger, pain, sensations of littleness, and feelings of death. If the therapist manages to draw near the dark, damp, and dirty places where feelings of disgust make life feel disgusting, where the networks of internal relations have been systematically torn apart, the patient acquires the ability to effect a split that can bring about differentiation between prisoner and gaoler, the first step towards getting one's self back and, despite one's wounds, taking up a place in life once again.

As Emma Bolshia Bravo says:

> To understand the importance of violence coming from the State, it is necessary to consider a preliminary aspect: the modern State potentially holds the legitimacy and legal monopoly of violence. Firstly this legitimacy demands that it should watch over the welfare of the citizen, guaranteeing the democratic rights which allow all people to decide about their individual and collective futures. Secondly, the monopoly is legal, because it should preserve human rights as the basis of justice and protection of all citizens (2003, p. 25).

If the state abuses the power that it has been given by law, it abuses its legitimacy by using the justice system, the police, and military force to infringe human rights and to inflict torture. Thus the state plays with the very base of human culture, and employs the most degrading forms of social and psychological infringement, which threaten to destroy human social organization. With Freud's (1913) masterpiece *Totem and Taboo*, this very fundamental theme concerning ethics and civilization was for the first time introduced to the psychoanalytic tradition, specifically with the myth of the Primitive Horde and its defeat, focusing on the complex construction of society.

When the state breaks with its function as social integrator, it returns to being a producer of barbaric conditions. As Bettelheim wrote in his testimonial book about concentration camps: "You can expect from a state that it guarantees the right to birth, the right to live in relative peace, the right not to be assassinated capriciously by the state and the right to feel that your life and physical integrity is being protected" (Bettelheim, 1952, translated from the Spanish version, 1981, p. 44).

Working with people affected by torture and state violence is working at the interface between psychotherapy, human rights, and politics. It is working in a space where neutrality is not possible, because it deals with transgressions which put the human condition in danger and which are rightly considered by international law as crimes against humanity.

Here politics are present as nowhere else, penetrating even the most private aspects of life. Through the torturer, a destructive external force invades the inner world. In the name of the state it destroys, without pity, the individual's psychic world, painstakingly constructed since childhood through education and culture.

Facing this work of traumatic destruction, the rule of abstinence in psychoanalytic treatment is necessary, but political neutrality is impossible. Moreover, there can surely be no greater duty for the psychoanalyst than to denounce such acts, and to refuse to remain silent in the face of such inhumanity.

PART I

FAR AWAY FROM HOME

CHAPTER ONE

Ambiguity as a defence in extreme trauma

Silvia Amati Sas

When we, as psychoanalysts, talk of the trauma that torture brings in its wake, we must remember that some of our customary premises, both theoretical and technical, may need to be modified when we are working with such patients. We have to bear in mind the fact that torture is an organized instrument of social and political power, the principal aim of which is to provoke catastrophic fear and traumatic consequences throughout an entire population. We should avoid the temptation of describing torture by means of what appear to be obvious concepts, such as sadomasochism, without taking into account the whole institutional context of required obedience and the authorization of acts of cruelty given to their agents by power entities.

Because social reality modifies subjectivity, we do not need to necessarily search in the patient's unconscious past for the determinant factors of the present traumatic situation. Specifically, at the beginning of the treatment, we should use our usual technique of the interpretation of transference very sparingly as this may create confusion before the patient has recovered his time and space orientation and his integrative capacities that have been altered by the traumatic events.

We share an important challenge with the patient who has suffered from social violence: to avoid unconscious adaptability, collusion, and complicity with the torturing system. In fact, social conformism is the aim of every system that bases its method of government on institutionalized violence as a means of obtaining submissiveness and avoiding public criticism or any form of rebellion. We have to challenge within ourselves our unconscious tendency towards "defensive ambiguity", a position of elasticity and malleability through which we can avoid inner conflict and criticism, and which may even lead us to consider as taken for granted what is in fact perverse. That is why it is of particular importance for us to be alert to the affective signals of subjective opposition to adaptability and imposed conformism, such as shame, despair, or indignation, be it in ourselves or in our patient (Amati Sas, 1989, 1992).

I use the word "challenge" deliberately, in order to make clear that psychic survival has ethical claims, which are legitimately aggressive! My intention here is to highlight those psychic mechanisms that imply a tacit acceptance of any situation or reality context, however unjust or illegal, by considering it as obvious, familiar, or banal and thus facilitating subjective conformism.

Since 1972, when I began treating Latin American victims of social and political trauma, it has become evident to me that to be able to treat these patients, we need psychoanalytic models that take into account the dynamic interplay between subjectivity and the contextual environment. Bleger's model of ambiguity (1972) has been of important conceptual help with this. I was later also able to "conjugate" these concepts with Puget's (1995) description of three "spaces of subjectivity", which are: intra-subjectivity, the relationship between ego and internal objects; inter-subjectivity, the relationship between self and other in external reality; and trans-subjectivity, the relationship between the self and the shared social context.

To put it briefly, "ambiguity" is the clinical expression of an "ambiguous nucleus", a residue of "primary non-differentiation" which remains in the mature personality. Bleger's (1972) premise is that this "ambiguous nucleus" is necessarily projected and placed through a "symbiotic link" in some external "depository". This unconscious but inevitable dependency on the external world provides the self with a feeling of security and a sense of belonging. If, because of external circumstances such as terrorism, the ambiguous nucleus loses its depositories, ambiguity is re-introjected, thereby giving rise to uncertainty, confusion, and various forms of anxiety: for example, panic, numbing, feelings of strangeness, and perplexity. A new symbiotic link is thus established immediately so that adaptation to new depositories, i.e. context and circumstances, sets in. Bleger uses the term "ambiguous position" to refer to a pre-conflictive, pre-paranoid-schizoid position, which must be clearly distinguished from ambivalence and contradiction, and which can operate as a defence.

When the conditions in the external world suddenly change in a traumatic manner, ambiguity becomes a major form of defence. The mimetic quality of ambiguity, thanks to its adaptability, and emotional numbing, protects the rest of the personality, which remains as if encapsulated and suspended. The dynamics of ambiguity allow us to imagine how intentionally provoked changes in the external world can reach the more intimate, vulnerable, and dependent aspects of subjectivity. Social reality actually functions as a "depository" for the uncertain and undifferentiated aspects of our subjectivity, whatever our chronological age, while social context silently provides and supports the illusion of belonging, safety, and certainty.

Traumatic social violence thus gives rise to adaptive subjective phenomena of obviousness and familiarity with the altered situation which is a "defence through ambiguity" and which may lead to an "adaptation to whatsoever". When a person is in a state of ambiguity, critical thinking and alarm mechanisms are altered, such that the individual and the group may become easily swayed.

In the psychotherapy of extreme situations, it is not only a matter of "making the unconscious conscious", or of "integrating dissociations", but also of making the trauma and its unconscious defences—fragmentation, dissociation, and adaptation—thinkable. We give the patient the opportunity to transform defensive ambiguity, the absence of conflict, into critical ambivalence and to transform alienation into judgement. Such alienation may be considered a modification of thought and affects, without the subject's awareness, brought about by the active will of someone else (Aulagnier, 1979).

During the working through of their traumatic experience, patients have to decode their distressing affects, their shame and catastrophic anxiety, loss of meaning, and distorted sense of self-identity; in addition they also have to become able to de-legitimize and oppose the violence experienced.

At an intra-subjective level, social violence induces defensive regression to a state of ambiguity; at an inter-subjective level, it engenders significant alterations in human relations and it introduces misunderstandings in the form of equivocation, paradox, and confusion, which may provoke unknowing compromise. Inter-subjective misunderstanding is unavoidable when traumatic violence occurs in the family or in society. An aspect of what Ferenczi (1932) called "confusion of tongues" is an equivocal understanding between people; it is representative of a lack of perception and judgement and loss of indignation that appears whenever there is a "defence through ambiguity" which does not allow us to perceive our own doubts about something that is happening, or to express our true alarm at the right moment.

Trans-subjectivity can be understood as the subjective sharing of a common context or a cultural framework, for example the prohibition of incest, or as the shared participation in institutions, the legal system, or the state, that provide basic concrete certainties. As regards affects, trans-subjectivity has to do with shared feelings and illusions of faith, e.g., safety, or of catastrophe, loss of faith (Eigen, 1985), in relation to either the persistence or the disappearance of a concrete environmental context or of a meaningful symbolic frame of reference. Traumatic social violence is always directed to trans-subjectivity because by modifying or destroying a shared contextual environment of safety, be it by naked terror or by other less perceptible means such as hunger or unemployment, it drives a whole population towards conformism, incapacity to criticize, suggestibility, and easy manipulation.

I would like to discuss some aspects of social violence from a clinical perspective with reference to Altea, a student who some twenty years ago campaigned against the repressive politics of the Latin American country where she was born. Altea "disappeared" and was tortured and imprisoned in a concentration camp for several months. Shortly after her release and subsequent exile in Europe, she began psychoanalytic psychotherapy with me that lasted for some ten years. Altea's example will help us to understand what I call "adaptation to whatsoever" and the complex relationship of the prisoner with the agents of the torture system, a relationship which all too easily we could think of as "identification with the aggressor".

From the beginning it was clear to me that Altea was alienated by one particular person in the camp, thanks to whom in her view she was still alive, someone who had very skilfully set himself up as a paternal transference figure. This "impostor" was an army officer, an intelligent manipulator, who was attracted by Altea's proud and haughty temperament in that it satisfied his need to dominate.

During her therapy, I could see Altea's inner struggle between her unconscious submission to, and at the same time, her resistance to the impostor. We must bear in mind that in a concentration camp, the prisoner's sense of identity is conditioned by the fact of belonging in such a perverse context. In spite of her efforts to "survive as a person" in that situation, there was in her an ambiguous "grey area" (Levi, 1986) of unconscious compromise and adaptation of which she was also ashamed.

Two years after the end of our regular sessions, Altea wanted to resume her psychotherapy because she realized that she "was letting other people do absurd things" to her without protesting as much as she ought; she saw this as a symptom that referred back to her concentration camp experience.

Since we no longer lived in the same town, we saw each other only from time to time. In her third session she brought a book, saying that "This time she had found what she was looking for"! The book was an account told by a woman about her marriage to an ex-Nazi doctor who, she came to realize, was maltreating her psychologically in a subtle manner, as he had already done with his former wives. She became aware of her alienation from him, and managed to break free from the situation. Altea handed me the book, in which she had underlined the word "infamy", and then read aloud an episode in which the main character was in an isolated place when someone she did not know struck her violently on the head. She would later die as a result of the trauma. At that very moment she thought: "No. No." I interpreted the "No. No" as what Altea had come to me to look for; the "No" that I had kept safe for her and that she had now managed to find by herself. It became evident to me that until that moment, Altea had not completely acknowledged her rejection and refusal of the torture situation. I had been the depository of her painful emotional distress and unthinkable experiences during all those years in which she had gradually worked through her experience of torture. My presence had given her the guarantee of her "No", which our working together represented for her. Certainly, that "No" was also mine, considering my constant "ethical alarm" (Amati Sas, 1994), and my effort to observe myself as a participant because in my innermost trans-subjectivity, I also belong to the dreadful humanity where such events can take place.

I have been the witness to Altea's process of transformation, her efforts to free herself of confusion and chaos, to separate out the different periods and places of her life, and to expel from her mind the parasitical world she had incorporated. In my counter-transference, I saw myself as the guarantor of the existence of an "original Altea" whose self-esteem had collapsed, forcing her to become a "concentration camp Altea". Together with my holding function, I interpreted for her, little by little, the significance and meaning of her dreams, thoughts, and memories, trying to follow the rhythm of her own insight into the tragic reality and the ghastly truth that she had experienced.

Altea's shame explains her inner conflict concerning her defensive ambiguity and her comparison of the different images she had of herself (Amati Sas, 1992). Several layers of shame reflected the infamies she had accepted and had adapted to, but it was only when she had already recovered her more mature levels of psychic functioning that she could represent, in dreams and memories, her most unbearable shame: the fact that she had been influenced in her behaviour and thinking by the concentration camp lifestyle. Sometimes, in her state of alienation, when she spoke about certain circumstances in which she had made concessions or had somehow participated in the military system, she would talk as if she had acted spontaneously; that is why her "No. No", and the inner struggle against infamy that she was now able to accept, were so important.

From the outset I could see that Altea was struggling against dissociation. On the one hand, she was true to herself, to her "identificatory project" (Aulagnier, 1979) and to her ideals of justice and authenticity; on the other, she was completely tied, in an alienated way, to the concentration camp way of life and to the impostor who, in her inner world, turned into a saboteur, a parasitical superego that imposed loyalty. The more ambiguous aspects of her personality, which were deposited in the perverse system, her "adaptation to whatsoever", gave obvious familiarity to the reality she had been forced to live through. I could see that to some extent she had been "impregnated" by the style of the military world; this became manifest in certain attitudes and in her sometimes haughty way of talking about other people. Altea seemed not to be aware of this unconscious imitation and involuntary obedience to the power system until she reached a later stage in her therapeutic process.

The impostor was a very commanding figure, especially in the initial stages of Altea's therapy. In order to fight against this agent of a violent system, the usurper of Altea's internal world, he had to be acknowledged as such and symbolically disarmed but he was still, alas, a dangerous character in external reality. Altea's relatives, who had remained in her country of origin, were constantly under threat via anonymous telephone calls: this permanent "state of menace" (Puget, 1986) from the torture system was intended to keep Altea's hands tied, no matter how far away she was. These worrisome threats to her family were constant reminders of the trauma she had been subject to. On a few occasions she went through a phase of intense panic in which she had hallucinations of the torturers, especially when she denounced them publicly and testified to what she had witnessed in the concentration camp.

The aim of a system of torture is to fragment the prisoner's feeling of continuity, sense of identity, and his capacity for comprehension and thinking by inducing confused perceptions and equivocal and paradoxical thoughts, with constant terror and loss of all external depositories from one's own clothing to the abolition of protective laws such as habeas corpus. That is why I think it is important not to offer early interpretations that would link the agents of violence to the patient's basic objects, her father or mother, or to the analyst and vice versa. Keeping the aggressive object clearly identified as such, and his influence somehow under control, becomes a process of dis-alienation and dis-identification that will gradually diminish his impact on the patient. At a later stage in the therapeutic process, it will be possible to interpret the patient's defensive style and the various transference aspects that emerge in the analytic situation.

Traumatic violence provokes a regression to a malleable and penetrable state of ambiguity which allows the torturer to impose himself on the inner world and to occupy the place of the victim's privileged objects, thereby usurping and sabotaging the victim's "identification project" (Aulagnier, 1979), the ideal moral functioning of the person: the Ego Ideal. In the state of immobile dependency produced in the prisoner, there is imprinting of the perverse external world, an adaptive remodelling which is unknown to the subject and makes him remain symbiotically dependent on the context, adopting a mentality which is not his own.

This could perhaps be called "identification with the aggressor", following Ferenczi's (1932) use of the term. The victim introjects the world of the concentration camp, or is introjected by it, and at the same time allows the aggressor to abuse his or her internal world. However, as Berenstein (2001) points out, external imposition is not identification. A regressive state of ambiguity facilitates introjection, incorporation, and internalization, while identification implies a more mature and differentiated functioning.

The therapist who is dealing with states of extreme violence cannot make any concession to the impostor; there is no reason here to accept the usurped transference. For the patient, the gradual moral condemnation and working through of inner compromises with the perverse situation are not limited to the actual period of therapy; they will reappear at various moments and in different circumstances of life as problems to be solved, along with the need to understand the political scenario which he or she had had to endure, in an ongoing existential process in working-through.

What is common to different traumatic situations is the "self-referential" attitude of the victim; victims feel themselves to be responsible for the violence that has been inflicted on them by someone else. Feeling responsible, however, is not the same as feeling guilty. We are responsible, in a sense intrinsic to the human condition, every time someone breaks "the rules that make us behave as human beings" (Bleger, 1970, in Kaes, 1987, p. 539) or when we experience the absence of "the mechanism through which we are able to confront another psychic life" (Freud, 1921, p. 298, footnote 2). Paradoxically, in the intra-subjective dimension, victims take upon themselves their aggressor's inability to feel compassion, empathy, or respect as the aggressor is still just another human being. The victims may even feel shame at the perpetrator's arrogance but on the inter-subjective level they may, defensively, try to appear just as indifferent or as cynical as the aggressor.

The emotional dilemma evoked by these simultaneous feelings, which are not the same as ambivalence, is compensated for by the secret internal concern for some other person, which represents an "object to be saved" (Amati Sas, 2004). Altea, for example, came to realize that while she was in the concentration camp, she had "put on hold" all mourning for her assassinated husband, but had often thought that "He was lucky not to have endured what she was experiencing". In the course of the therapeutic process, when she was able to recall this secret concern for her husband's dignity, she realized that during her imprisonment she had not lost, as she thought, her sense of ethical continuity. Her husband was her "object to be saved", the representation of a link in which there is no room for betrayal, the illusion of an authentic and non-alienating relationship.

There is always an "object to be saved" in the therapeutic process of patients who have been maltreated and abused; it represents the inner link with some other person whose fate and dignity have preoccupied the patient. We can consider this as the secret expression of the "critical opposition" to aggression and enslavement which, as Ferenczi (1932) points out, we can find in every person who has been made a victim. Even if it has been forgotten or repressed, this concern for another is the prisoner's secret challenge in the face of the alienating situation.

In concluding this paper, I would like to discuss the feeling of "indignation" as a factor that sets itself up against alienation and compromise. Just as in the case of "shame", the sense of "indignation" can be seen as the signal of an unconscious subjective conflict relating to our ambiguity, our tendency to "take for granted" or "turn a blind eye" (Steiner, 1985) to conflictive social and political realities.

When, as psychoanalysts, we are faced with dramatic clinical experiences of political torture, it is not hate nor the wish for revenge that comes to mind; we feel indignation. Theoretically, indignation can be seen as a "working-off mechanism" (Bibring, quoted by Laplanche, 1993), an emotion, an emotional impulse that helps us move out of the immobility, perplexity, confusion, and fear that overwhelm us when we realize that another human being is motivated by a destructive intent. It signals the fact that we are in contact with an abusive reality. The feeling of indignation necessarily has an aggressive dimension, that of an impulse that helps us to prioritize our values and free up our ability to think critically, as well as our capacity to choose and to make a "judgement of condemnation".

Indignation is based on the ethical need for trust, truth, and faith. That is why, with such patients, it is extremely important to take into consideration all the transference and counter-transference feelings of indignation in our joint struggle against torture. It is essential to maintain alive the feeling of indignation within ourselves, because in contemporary society, dominated by mass media, everything, including torture, can be made to seem both acceptable and justifiable. With patients who have been abused, or subject to torture, paedophilia, prostitution, or rape, we struggle jointly in their private inner world against certain aspects of society that tend towards the disappearance of the prohibition of incest as an organizer of society.

Dominated as it is by the media where all is permitted, contemporary society tends to push both indignation and shame into the background. With the excessive and equivocal dissemination of images of torture, for example, we end up by adapting to it; overloaded and indifferent, we may lose all sense of indignation.

There can be no doubt that all the laws, treaties, and institutions which condemn torture and seek to prevent it, even if they are not complied with, do offer public guarantees that provide the necessary trans-subjective "holding" for the private and intimate dimension of our therapeutic work.

CHAPTER TWO

Routes to the unspeakable: working with victims of torture

Mary Raphaely

Introduction

Our post-modern world is littered with displacement and dispersal; most of us engaging in attempts at reconstruction, reframing what has gone before. But the task for refugee victims of torture is altogether different. The shards of memory which pierce their lives make such reconstruction deeply dangerous. How can one find the courage to face the unspeakable? How can healing begin?

What follows is an amalgamation of papers presented at the EFPP conferences in Lisbon (2004) and Dresden (2005), where I participated in the ongoing workshop on Torture and State Violence. Here, I record some of my experience as a group analytic psychotherapist working with the Medical Foundation for the Care of Victims of Torture in London, a human rights organization enabling survivors of torture and organized violence to engage in a healing process.

The Foundation adopts a holistic approach. Treatment goes hand in hand with casework as specialist staff assist clients with practical problems such as homelessness and destitution.

Counselling a survivor of torture and organized violence is at the interface of an individual's internal and external world; practitioners

13

have to incorporate and integrate references to both. We offer a wide range of clinical and other services but, most important of all, the Medical Foundation is a place where survivors can feel that their experiences are recognized and accepted, and can safely express their grief and anger.

In Britain, our asylum process is so protracted that clients frequently speak of the psychological torture they continue to live through. The fantasy of having finally reached safety in England is quickly shattered, especially since the recent London bombings. These have had a devastating effect on our clients, and have greatly increased hostility towards those from abroad.

It is political systems rather than therapy which lead to regression in our clients. It is thus vital to retain a strong pragmatic approach, to help clients to re-engage with their adult egos and get back in touch with reality. Clients do not come to the Foundation to sort out their psychopathology; they need to address the sequelae of torture and organized violence. However, there is generally a correlation between the experience of internalized positive objects and the capacity for healing.

While cognizant of the crucial importance of early relationships on the internal world, I question whether a strictly Eurocentric Western analytical model is always the appropriate approach, working across cultures and frequently across languages.

As practitioners, how do we go about healing a broken spirit? I have not found it helpful in this work to remain too entrenched in orthodoxy. My group analytic training and experience provide a fundamental framework, but I have learned to make many adaptations.

Furthermore, how indeed do we protect ourselves, while being constantly confronted by human cruelty and destruction?

Non-verbal or pre-verbal therapy

Part of my work at the Foundation takes place in a beautiful, very contained garden in north London, where I run the Natural Growth Project. My clients here are extremely fragile, those who feel completely overwhelmed and who need to engage initially with a less verbal form of therapy. The model I work with involves a way of being, without words, akin to a pre-verbal state; after a time, people progress through this stage and are able to confront more directly and work through their experiences. Thus our work is an early stage on the journey to recovery and autonomy.

Although I often see clients for individual sessions initially, I believe that group work is an essential part of the recovery process. The group offers the possibility of a new homeland, a secure base; it becomes a psychic container.

As a result of their brutal and horrifying experiences, our clients are trapped in a malignant matrix. It is important to explore together how their terrible experiences restrict and influence their lives today, and to struggle to make sense together of the senseless. Many of our groups are conducted in languages more familiar to the clients than English, sometimes with interpreters. Thus they constitute a kind of homeland where there is, by language alone, a kind of instant belonging. Many of our clients come from cultures which depend more on collective than individual identity.

It is particularly important, as soon as it is appropriate, to place clients who are survivors of rape in a group with others who have suffered a similar fate, rather than working individually with them. Almost 100% of our female clients are rape victims but there are a good many men too.

Generally, I am committed to working with mixed gender groups. They offer a vital space in which men and women, so damaged by their experiences, can slowly renegotiate their relationship with the other sex. However, the timing of entry into such groups must be handled with great care.

It can initially be very complicated for women who have been raped to be in the company of men. They appear to have the more difficult task, as they have suffered so greatly at the hands of men. However, the need to protect the men sometimes emerges, as the women unite.

Generally men are more easily able to express anger and are more strongly in touch with their own potential strength. The women seem more lost and disconnected. The men are more likely to have had direct political engagement in their countries, and suffered the consequences, whereas the women frequently were tortured because of their association with their men. The lack of a direct connection between action and consequence increases their feelings of living in a senseless world.

At the Natural Growth Project we use nature as a metaphor for life, and as a way of reaching and healing the soul. The work is constantly about seeking links between nature and the inner landscape, combining horticultural work with psychotherapy. Somehow, the capacity to symbolize in the context of the natural world appears to remain intact, despite the terrible damage inflicted by torture. We draw on a very primal connection; everyone, wherever they are from and however they grew up, will have had some relationship with nature. With its very early origins, this is unlikely to have been contaminated by external events.

The traumatic loss of the motherland casts the refugee adrift; working with the earth can therefore be a vital grounding experience. The cycles of life, death, and rebirth are evident in the sowing of seeds, the growth, harvesting, and dying back which nature provides.

Plants are highly evocative, providing an instant link to the past. I often see a look of painful recognition as a client stoops to smell a flower; this can be the vital missing key, breaching a well-constructed wall of defence. It could take years to reach this point of memory in a conventional group, particularly with the degree of trauma we frequently encounter. Thus nature provides a continuum between a client's pre- and post-traumatic states. For so many, torture is experienced as a rupture which they cannot reach behind, disrupting the core of their identity.

In the autumn we enter a time of dying back, of cold and darkness. This reflects physically the internal state of many clients, who find themselves acutely sensitive to the darkening days. For many, their torture took place at night and the darkness is terrifying. We work on bringing plants to shelter in our greenhouse, where they will have extra protection; we use this to explore what coming to the project might mean for our clients.

In cutting back dead vegetation, we talk with the clients about the need to shed those parts of life which have died and which encumber us, preventing new growth. We put these cuttings on the compost heap, talking about how, by turning them over, they will eventually provide nourishment for the garden in the future. Perhaps if our clients can eventually confront some of their experiences, they will provide a kind of strength and wisdom with which to move forward. This opens the door to mourning for the lost self, as well as grief for lost loved ones.

Seeds are a vital part of the work. Also in the autumn, we gather dried seed heads from the garden, storing them safely indoors until the time is right to plant them and watch the new life grow. Many clients are for a time unable to plant seeds; they cannot imagine the future at all.

Horrific experiences block thinking, emphasize dissociation, and prevent healing. Torture destroys, fragmenting the psyche and the soul.

In the wasteland left behind, it becomes crucial to find small signs of life, of hope. Nature provides many possibilities and the Natural Growth Project offers a transitional space in which to explore these. Some illustrations of our work follow.

Case study 1: Suzi

Suzi presented as a very disturbed 45-year-old woman from east Africa. Limping severely, she smiled continuously even when tears rolled down her cheeks. As tiny children, she and her twin sister had been abandoned by their mother into the care of their father. Brought up by a disapproving stepmother, they only occasionally experienced the protective intervention of their father. Related to a dictator, from childhood she was surrounded by murder and death. She had a strong sense of her own malignant power; her torture has confirmed her early phantasies.

She had suffered abduction, rape, and torture. Her teenage children had been seized by the same faction as her captors, before her own capture, and their whereabouts remain unknown. Her twin sister has been killed.

Taken captive to marshlands with many other women, she was beaten continuously, raped, and forced to look after the rebels. She both suffered and witnessed many terrible things and she was forced to spend most of her time in the water. Today she suffers from severe arthritis.

Early in her individual therapy, as we walked in the manicured London garden, she talked of protecting me in case the rebels should come. She could not look at our fish-pond; for many months this water remained terrifying to her. Her internal and external worlds were merged.

Suzi told me that she was now, at all times, accompanied by her dead twin. One day she explained that she had wanted to cut off her two big toes, as they were rotting from all the water. She was prevented by the thought that I would not be pleased. I referred her to one of our psychiatrists, who prescribed some medication, and we continued our work in the garden.

Suzi wanted to grow peanuts, as she had back home. She brought some raw nuts, and started them off in pots in the greenhouse. When they had grown sufficiently she put them in the garden. Exposed to the

English weather, they died. I was concerned at what the effect on her might be, but this occurrence became a turning point.

A couple of weeks later, she came to her session and described how she had found herself sitting on her fourth floor window ledge in south London, where she lives. She was ready to jump, because someone, actually her case worker, was knocking on her door insistently. She was convinced it was the rebels. But then she remembered her peanut plants; they had not survived because of the English weather. This reminded her that she was in London and the panic passed.

I suggested Suzi join a library. Later she told me that when she reached the library it was filled with black men. She panicked, believing that she saw the rebels among them, and ran away. This led to much work between us on her notion that all white people were good and all black people were bad.

We gave her a small patch of the garden to cultivate by herself. She insisted on fencing it in with bamboo; life was too dangerous to leave her plants unprotected. Many months later we were able to celebrate her removing this fence and starting to work in the larger garden.

After about a year I placed her in a mixed gender and heterogeneous group, with people from Ethiopia, Congo, Rwanda, and Russia. Initially extremely resistant to the idea, within a month she became a regular and contributing member. Since then Suzi has enrolled at an adult education college full of students of mixed gender and race. She also now works part-time as a volunteer for a refugee organization and she is clear that this would have been impossible before her time in the group.

Eventually Suzi was granted full refugee status. Recently she told the group that when she received the papers informing her of this, she withheld the information for weeks. It felt like the end of the world; she thought she would no longer qualify for treatment with me.

Suzi still occasionally spends whole days "on the buses" as she puts it, touring London in the slim hope that she will see her children by chance. Around these times, she sinks into deep depression, eating little and retreating into her room.

A conventional approach would have been of limited use in the early stages of her journey. It is clear that her unstable internal structure greatly restricts her capacity for recovery. But it is equally clear that to some degree she needs to retain her state. If Suzi were to think coherently for any length of time, she would have to face the likely fate of her children. Agonizingly, she knows the probabilities only too well.

Perhaps Suzi is behaving appropriately for what she has to live with. Perhaps we need to accept and celebrate the extent of her recovery as far as it has gone. Probably she will need the link with the Foundation for some time to come, and perhaps in time she will be able to confront more directly the realities of her existence.

Case study 2: Hassan

Hassan is a 35-year-old Kurdish man who has suffered horrific torture. He was referred to me by a clinical psychologist at the Foundation, who felt that individual therapy was no longer helpful. She believed that Hassan, formerly a farmer, had a very strong connection with nature and could benefit from joining the Natural Growth Project.

He arrived at his first session three hours early. He told me that he had been in hospital and that he would come back at the correct time. He returned half an hour late but the interpreter booked to assist me had failed to appear.

I started working with him alone, sitting inside. A small and extremely tense man, he clenched his jaw, the muscles in his face working continuously. To everything I asked, he stated, "Do not remember." It quickly became clear that we would not get very far, so I proposed walking in the garden.

Hassan walked ahead of me down the steps onto the lawn, and breathed deeply. I asked him why he had been in hospital. He said, "I am now living there, I cannot remember for how long. I could not control myself, I was shouting and throwing things, and trying to kill myself." I asked what he did all day; he answered that now he was given a lot of medicine, and he slept most of the time. This was delivered in a monotone voice without any eye contact.

How was he feeling out here, I asked. He said that it felt like something was going to explode inside him all the time; for this reason he could not trust himself, and was in hospital.

At this point the interpreter arrived and I suggested that we walk further into the garden. As we did so, Hassan walked away from us, tears rolling down his cheeks. After a couple of minutes I asked him what was happening; he said, "I do not remember." I waited, and then he said, "Sometimes inside I cannot breathe, I feel locked in … but here it is different outside."

I asked if there were any plants here that he knew from his country. He said, "I do not remember." I asked what work he used to do before and he told me that he was a farmer. How big was his farm? "I do not remember." What did you used to grow there? "I do not remember."

I wondered aloud if the medication made it harder for him to remember. "I do not know," he replied. I suggested that perhaps when he was assaulted in his country, he had suffered some blows to the head? Hassan nodded. And perhaps also there are so many things that he had tried hard to forget, that he could not remember most things? For the first time he looked at me and said, "Yes, this is very true."

Now we walked into the Healing Garden, where we grow plants for use in our herbal clinic. I explained this, and asked him if in his country, plants were used for medicine: "I do not remember." As we walked towards the greenhouse, he volunteered, "You are right to be working outside. Nature is beautiful; it will never hurt you like men do. This is a good place."

We went into the greenhouse, where a large basket of small, unripe green figs had been left. I took a few in my hand and said, "We picked these last week. They never ripened; they never became what they might have been, because they are perhaps in the wrong place. In your country they would have grown big and delicious to eat, no?" He was watching me intently as I went on, "Perhaps this is a little bit how you feel about yourself, Hassan?" He smiled for the first time, "This is exactly so."

Now I turned to a box of drying nasturtium capers. Holding some in my hand I told him, "We picked these from the plant a few weeks ago. Now is the time when they are drying; it is not the time for them to grow, it is the quiet time." Hassan said, "They are locked in their hard shells." I asked if this was how he felt also. He smiled, "It is so." I said we both knew that after this dry time, there would be new growth. He said, "Inshallah."

I asked Hassan if he would like to have some of these seeds; he brightened visibly and I gave him some. He carried them cupped in his hands like the treasure that they represented for him. I suggested that perhaps when he felt a bit better he would like to come back, when the time was right, and plant them with me. He said, "Yes, I want to do that, but now I cannot trust myself; I have to be in the hospital."

As we walked back to the house, he kept looking at his seeds, and smiling. Then he asked when he could come again. I said that he could come back soon, when he felt better. He said, "I want to do that. This pressure inside me, that makes me want to explode, it is already a little bit less."

Passing a lavender bush, I picked a little and explained that if he put it under his pillowcase, he might find it helped him to sleep. He thanked me. As we were going inside, Hassan said to the interpreter, "This woman has changed everything completely today." I smiled and said it was the garden which had done this. He nodded.

Inside, we carefully put his seeds in an envelope and wrote his name on it. He thanked me and shook my hand. As I walked him to the door he took my hand again and held it. I repeated that when he was feeling better and the time was right, we would plant the seeds together here. He smiled, "Inshallah."

The session had lasted only 35 minutes.

After some individual work, Hassan felt well enough to join a men's gardening group, preferring not to engage further with psychotherapy. He has become an actively engaged and contributing member. In recent months he has been joined by his wife and children and he has reassumed responsibility as father of his family.

It is clear to me that at the point we met, the traumatic events of Hassan's life had completely overwhelmed his capacity to care for himself and he was in extreme need of the kind of intervention that the Natural Growth Project offers. In time, it allowed him to move towards recovery, working in a language that he understood deeply.

Case study 3: Rosa

Rosa is a 33-year-old woman from West Africa; she is tall and well built. She presented with a defeated air, keeping her head bowed and constantly looking ashamed; she found it virtually impossible to express herself verbally. She spoke very little English but good French.

How to begin, with so little verbal communication? In addition to being deeply traumatized by her torture, Rosa was locked into virtual silence by her grief and shock at the loss of her twin brother in violent circumstances, about eighteen months previous to our meeting.

She made it clear to me that being born a twin was at the core of her identity and that in her society this had particular significance: she and her brother were regarded and treated as special. It was essential to attempt an understanding of this from within her cultural framework, and explore the impact of the dreadful events upon her.

Rosa had witnessed a violent confrontation between the police and her brother's organization, after which he disappeared. He was never seen again and she believes that he was killed, although she never found his body. Her attempts to establish what happened to him had led to her detention and torture. As his twin, there were essential rituals she wanted to perform in burying him; she was never able to do this.

Rosa was arrested and over the next months she was beaten, burnt with cigarettes, and raped frequently. This terrible treatment continued, usually at night. Several months later she was hospitalized. From there she eventually escaped, travelled to Britain, and sought asylum.

At our first meeting, I was forcibly struck by Rosa's bizarre manner of communication. Sunk into her own thoughts, she volunteered very little; it was as if she found verbal communication unnecessary. When I asked a question, she seemed to expect me to know the answer. At night she had terrible nightmares and flashbacks. She suffered from constant and crippling headaches. She hardly slept and was frequently dizzy and vomiting. Indeed, she feared sleep because of the horrors it would bring.

It was immediately clear that Rosa was happiest outside. In the Healing Garden, amongst the plants grown for herbal remedies, she spoke freely for the first time, of a special plant medicine for inherited illnesses. Her grandmother had taught her to prepare this. She also told me that there was a tree special to twins, and that she had seen it in my office; she had recognized it by its shape. She called it the Peace Tree— L'Arbre de Paix—and she insisted on watering it before she left.

For her second session, Rosa took herself straight out to a bench in the Healing Garden; we held her session there. She reported that she had been granted refugee status but she seemed unaware of the enormous importance of this.

Did she now feel she had control over any aspect of her life, or was able to make any choices? She smiled and shrugged. I offered her the garden shears and suggested that she prune an overgrown shrub to the shape she wanted. She found this difficult, and kept checking for my approval. Soon, however, she became lost in the task and relaxed. When she had finished, I commented that she had made some decisions here, and slowly she could begin to do so in the rest of her life.

Rosa arrived three hours early for her third session and disappeared into the garden. At the appointed time, I found her asleep on a bench in the Healing Garden. She said she had slept well and completely without fear. As she dozed among the lavender and the bees, she felt that she was back in her village.

She spoke about how she and her brother had communicated all their lives without words and they had never really needed anyone else; the family had called them witches. Now she felt that half of her was not there any more, although her brother talked with her all the time.

Rosa said she had often thought of killing herself. Passing many days without eating, she dreamt of her brother beckoning her. She told me that in her country it is very common for the second twin to die soon after the first, just to waste away.

Now she spoke of some of the special customs for twins. When a mother gives birth to twins, she is presented with the Peace Tree, which is kept in the house for the twins. If they become too excitable, they are stroked with a leaf or given the fruit to eat.

It had been her brother's task to tend the plant. Now Rosa wanted to water the plant in my office. It is worth noting that the plant Rosa spoke of had been pruned by us to a shape which is not its natural form. It could not therefore be the tree she had known, but was obviously close enough to what she held in her mind that it facilitated her ready transference.

As she watered this tree, Rosa talked quietly in her own language; she told me that she was asking her brother for advice. Over the next months, whether or not she watered the tree became an important indicator, but my understanding of its significance changed. Initially I felt that she had slipped backwards and was lost, trying to anchor herself. Later I came to believe that taking over her brother's role in tending the tree was enormously important; she was reclaiming some of the power that he had held in their twinship.

Over the next three months I saw Rosa fortnightly. In my office she remained almost silent; outside, she slipped into something deeply familiar and was able to speak more freely.

She remained petrified of the dark and full of dread of the impending winter. Very afraid of people, she talked almost exclusively to the Moroccan children of the family where she was living, and to me. Still filled with feelings of shame about her rape, she was convinced that it was obvious to all who met her.

In time, I proposed that Rosa join a women's group conducted by me. At the first session she began to weep silently. To the group she said, "They only need to know that I am a twin."

After some weeks one of the women in the group was very upset, crying loudly. There was a striking gesture by Rosa, who took her hand hesitantly and then rubbed it gently in comfort. She told us she had found a new place to live. But she only slept there at night, returning to the Moroccan family during the day because she could not bear the solitude. Would she like to tell the group more about why she felt the solitude so badly? Softly, she said, "I am not ready."

Rosa started attending only alternate sessions; perhaps she could not tolerate any more. I believe it was extraordinarily difficult for her to form a relationship after the death of her twin; to do so would constitute a betrayal. She was struggling with increased engagement.

When we saw Rosa again, she was tearful, describing a terrible pain in her breast. She was feeling weak and giddy and terribly sad. The Moroccan family had moved, so she had lost the place she went every day to escape her solitude.

After she missed two sessions the group was delighted when she returned. She did not say much but often nodded empathically. When she was pressed to speak, she said that she took medicine to try to help the pain but that her heart was broken. The tablets calmed her pain, but they did not heal it. She still thought constantly about her brother and her three children.

Rosa spoke of how in the beginning, when she first arrived in England, she had always felt frightened, and had hidden herself, but this had changed with her time in the group; she had begun to speak a little here.

Her grandmother had told her that her twin was always with her and that when a man and a woman are together as twins, it is the man who directs. She went on to say that all her scars were a daily reminder of the killing of her brother; they also reminded her of her sacrifice for him. This was a very significant moment. Her guilt was beginning to turn to anger at his abandonment of her.

Now Rosa became very distressed, and wept. She pushed attempts to comfort her aside, and said, "Nobody can understand it ... we grew together, we lived together ... I want to accept that my brother is dead, but because I do not know, I think that I am not ready to do this. I feel that half of me is gone. The scar begins to heal but it begins to bleed again if it is touched at all."

We asked Rosa to think about what she would like to share with us about the burial rites for twins in her country. Perhaps, when she was ready, we could conduct a symbolic ritual in the garden. She smiled, nodded, and then disappeared for three weeks.

When she reappeared, she had restyled her hair. She was standing up straighter, talking more English, making proper eye contact and smiling a lot more. She was determined to continue at college studying English, and then to find work.

Today, half a year later, she has finally succeeded in bringing her children to England. For the moment, she seems to have forgotten all about the *Arbre de Paix*, her Peace Tree. Or perhaps she has left it deliberately in my care, holding as it does the delusional parts of her.

Rosa and I began our relationship in French, the language of her country's colonizers. This would have influenced her ready transference as for a time I was all-powerful; by the end of the first session she had identified me as the keeper of her Peace Tree. Did a shift occur as she learnt some English and we began to communicate in a language that constitutes her future? Did this facilitate her emerging independence?

Conclusion

At the core of our work is the need to reach across frozen terrified space and begin to effect a thaw. I have learned that there are many different ways of doing this and that it is vital to stay open to whatever the needs of our clients might be.

A consequence of torture is that a very basic trust in the goodness of the world itself is shattered; how long it will take to redevelop will depend in part on the client's internal objects. Nature offers an unwavering predictability, with its inevitable cycles of growth and dying back. This becomes a steady template against which a client can begin to recreate order and meaning in his or her internal world.

People who have been shattered by traumatic events have an extreme need for psychic containment. It is as if the protective shield of Mother Nature offers an embrace which can transcend the trauma, allowing a deeply peaceful external space in which the internal transformation can begin. Here it is possible to nurture the small shoots of new life, growing from the stump of the amputations which have occurred.

The client's response is not, however, always a serene one; the directness with which this approach can breach defences can be extremely frightening. However, what is on offer is the possibility of reconnecting with the natural order of things, after the utter devastation which assails the lives of most of our clients.

The very strong transference to me is connected also to the protective functions of the organization, and to the garden itself. This can lead to a protracted engagement, but it is vital to help clients process what is happening, and to access the adult parts of themselves.

As one who conducts conventional analytic groups at the Medical Foundation as well as working on the Natural Growth Project, I know that for some clients this approach is a vital first step. They are too damaged and too fragile to be able to engage initially with a strictly verbal therapy. They very much need the transitional space we offer.

On a personal level, I know that I too am nourished and helped in this difficult work by working in the garden. Being in nature feeds the soul.

The last word should be given to a client, who said:

"Coming to work on the land feels like coming to see my mother; putting my hands in the soil feels like greeting a very old friend. This is my place of safety."

CHAPTER THREE

Social conflicts and psychic suffering

Anna Sabatini Scalmati

I have been involved for years in psychoanalytic psychotherapy with sub-Saharan Africans who have had experiences involving imprisonment, torture, and physical and sexual violence. At a time of absolute danger, they found themselves in the situation of having to choose between two alternatives: either give themselves up to a cruel and anonymous death, or escape, who cares to where. A strange quirk of fate made escape, and thus their arrival in Italy, possible.

Apart from brutality and violence, these people are burdened by the laceration of their social and family fabric, the warp and weft that weaves together their affective identity and their personality. In the past, state-sponsored terrorism covered them with ignominy and degradation. Today, a different social context is failing to recognize their needs thus they are destined to a precarious life of marginalization.

Clinical case history

I received a file from the institution I work with, giving me an outline of the situation of a 17-year-old boy who has accepted the advice of a social worker to talk to me. In this file I find that the boy spent many months in prison on account of his parents' political activity. Thanks to the help of others, he then managed to escape.

When state-sponsored violence puts a name on a blacklist, sooner or later family members, no matter whether they are adults or children, will be persecuted. The destiny of this boy, whom I will call Carlo, is no different to that of many others. Nothing is known about his family members.

After his escape, Carlo was put on a plane and sent to Italy: Fiumicino airport. As soon as they arrived, the "passer" accompanying Carlo vanished. Carlo was literally abandoned, at the mercy of a completely unknown and unpredictable context. In his pocket he had the equivalent of five dollars.

In addition to the catastrophic loss of his entire known world, family members, friends, peer group, and later prison, there was the terrible anxiety of the totally new and the total lack of any reference point. Bonds which are suddenly broken open up terrible wounds and create difficulties in distinguishing between past and present, between the inner and the outer world.

At his first appointment, indeed at all of them, Carlo arrives on time. He comes in shyly, his head down. I find it hard to recognize the adolescent described in his file. In my room he sits down, his head bent right down onto his chest. The only part of his face I can see is his right eyelid, which is lowered and pulsing, and his upper lip, which is also trembling.

The minutes go by in silence; only his body, closed in on itself, is communicating something. His hands are clasped together, his grip tightening; a pallor in his skin makes it look green and shadowy.

Closed in on himself, Carlo seems to be defending himself against a space with no limits into which he could be sucked and from which anything could appear. I try to contain the space for him with my eyes, and with my attention, which has in the meantime become very intense. After a while I tell him that I am with him in this space and that in this room we could do something together to help him. I tell him I know he has suffered a great deal.

After more than 30 minutes, he utters his first difficult words: he asks me for some water. Electric shock treatment makes you very thirsty. I go back and sit down and ask myself whether my eyes blanketing him, the silence in the room, the water I have given him, whether these things help him distinguish this place from the other places where he has been shut in for so long.

I see him struggle not to break down and weep, then, suddenly, two huge tears ooze out of his eyes, as big as snow drops.

It's dangerous to make a noise in prison, even more dangerous to show your pain. He has learnt to hold back his tears, to hide them, to condense them all into two huge drops. But it is also dangerous to be in contact with the anxiety that this room has brought out. It's important to mobilize this anxiety and keep it under control.

A few minutes before the end of the session I tell him that we've almost finished and that, if he agrees, we could meet at the same time, on the same day next week. He gets up. After a few seconds, without looking at me, but opening up his inner world to me, he says, "How can one be cured of all this ...?"

I say I do not know, but that together we can try.

During the session, his body, which had become a vehicle for strong emotions, had pushed his words away. But the strong sensation of oppression I feel at my temples gives me the measure of the intensity of the affective elements that had transited there.

This therapy will require a great deal of experience and clinical sensitivity; it seems more a matter of communication of transference and counter-transference than of interpretation of meanings.

The next week he comes punctually and continues to do so for the next two years.

At our first meeting, Carlo taught me that silence is a language in which many of our deepest communications take place. His silence, his body language, his immobile and trembling posture, the tension with which he clasps his hands, or, on cold days, the little hat on his bowed head, the distance he places between himself and the table, all these things give expression to his state of mind.

My room is small, cosy, and welcoming. And yet I have a sensation of cold, and the impression that the confines of my body encounter a vacuum. I let the minutes go by in silence and allow my feelings to decant. Gradually, I start talking to him about them. I talk about how he feels alone, or rather, isolated. About how the gap between his story and that of all the other people he meets makes him feel even more isolated. About how nothing around him makes sense. About how maybe he feels darkness around him and a lot of confusion. About how suffering these things together will slowly help him.

After a while, his head still bowed, he says, "My bones will never warm up again, my hands hurt, the blood does not flow." Rolling down his face, one, at maximum, two tears.

We have to gradually melt his world iced over with hatred, shame, and the pain of torture. We have to help his blood to flow in a body that has stared death in the face more than once. His nights are iced over too. He has not dreamed at night for months. He hardly sleeps; he is scared of his room mates.

Nights in prison are more dangerous than days. Free will is darker, more arbitrary. You are called, taken away; you never know whether you are coming back.

The sessions go on in more or less the same way; a few significant movements and a lot of silence. After two months, he manages to untie his hands, and his right hand goes up to his lips. A gesture to placate his terror, to feel himself, or simply a liberation? I do not know. It's a move, a hint of melting. After a while he says, "I can't manage to talk. I'm still there. What happened there is my present."

The pain that comes suddenly into your life makes the fear of aggression go on for ever. Time closes itself up into a continuous present. This stops him from going to see a doctor. He's afraid of his verdict: HIV infection. It also stops him from turning his voice into words, and from turning Carlo into a human being among other human beings rather than a "thing" in the hands of his prison keepers.

I tell him that I know it is hard to talk to an outsider about the pain, the shame, and the suffering that his young life has been subject to. I tell him that I am there to support him and help him with his difficulties, to relieve his experience of suffering and fear. I am there to help him feel that this is a different place, where he can begin to feel new days taking the place of his past. I am there to help him heal his wounds and start building the scar-tissue.

A typical mark of state-sponsored terrorism is the terrible fragility it leaves in its wake, an invasive sensation of being small and insignificant. A teenager whose adolescence has been violently ripped from him learns to live with these wounds, knows how to move, and what is in store. To open up in this country which is so different from his own, to find out what has happened to his family, perhaps completely wiped out, to look at his present life, this present life that has been forced onto him, opens up other wounds. He is scared; he does not know yet how big they are or how much they will cost him.

All this must be dealt with, but all in good time. First, it is imperative that Carlo perceives that there is somebody to share his fears, grasp his suffering, and help him to differentiate between the various aspects of his experience. It is vital that Carlo can deposit his shame, anger, pain, hatred, and death experiences in our meetings.

In the course of our sessions I am witness to the battle that the ice, his distrust, and the enormity of the facts engage with his words. I speak to him about this in very simple terms. He says, "The words come to my mouth, but then they go back again, they can't come out." I say this happens because they are not just words but screams, weeping, unadulterated emotions, cruel and concrete facts which are impossible to name. For a second, shyly, for the first time in months, he looks up at me. On his face there is a tear; on mine there is one too.

The next session he comes late. He says that he got off at the usual bus stop but that he got lost. He realized that he had been going round and round my building without recognizing the front door.

It's hard to re-establish trust, to go back to seeing the light. In just a few seconds you can face death, relationships are severed. If you try and climb up over the pile of rubble where evil has planted its flag and give some sense to your life, re-appropriating some kind of feeling, then you tend to lose your way; the path is slow, slippery, and hard to relate to real life.

After four months he manages to go to see a doctor, and then he has his first dream. It was terrible, so terrible that it hurts his heart. The dreams of these patients are so real that they have physical repercussions on their health.

"I saw my mother being massacred ... (silence) ... *effrayant!* I woke up with a gasp, it was terrible, my heart ... (he brings his hand to his chest) ... it hurts."

I ask myself to what psychic movement this dream owes its origins. What happened? What caused this melting, however painful it has been? I ask him about his day, about his evening. "I woke up to go to the bathroom. I was going back to my room when some men who live in the hostel, maybe they had been drinking, started being rude about Africa, laughing. Is it true, they asked me, that in your country men and women go around naked? I felt offended, I felt pain, I started defending my country, my land, and then I went away. I had never spoken with them; it hurt me a lot to hear what they were saying. Then I went to sleep, and then I had this dream."

I tell him that he had defended his community, that he had made an important distinction between the population and the prison-keepers. But his past, the violence of power, had become over-bearing, capturing him in its network of death where differences, contradictions, and ambivalence are wiped clean.

Before, I told him, it had been difficult for him to talk to the others in the hostel because his prison extended to the outside world. Now that he had succeeded in containing it within himself, now that he had had the courage to defend himself, to give his version of the facts, the soldiers had come back to get him, ready, with all their power, to hurt him in the heart.

As the weeks pass, Carlo slowly starts to reduce his defences. He stops immobilizing his anxieties in an autistic prison and starts coming into contact with his resources. He starts dreaming again. But his dreams are terrible. "It is night, dark. In the forest I am chased by soldiers who grab people and throw them into the flames." Another: "Soldiers are throwing prisoners from helicopters into the mouths of crocodiles."

When he has these dreams, he wakes up suddenly and then cannot go back to sleep.

Re-activating his dream activity goes hand in hand with a marked psycho-physical deterioration. In sessions, just a few, intense communications. Carlo is very pale, he feels ill, he has lost hope that he will ever come out of his confusion and fear, and yet he has started being more present during these days. Though only for brief moments, the past starts to become the past. During the day he is involved in his work, he feels a little safer at the hostel, but his nightmares have opened up the doors of hell. It seems as if what has not been killed in the past must be killed now. His rays of hope, though weak, have faded. I feel sorry for him.

One day he comes in limping. After a few minutes of silence, I ask him what happened to his leg. "They hit me." I am about to express my indignation and alarm when I realize that he is trying to say something. I give him time. After a while, he says, "Last night I had a terrible dream. I am in prison, the soldiers come in with pistols, guns, they hit me, and they kick me. I beg for mercy, but nothing, more kicks, punches; it wouldn't stop. Then a woman comes in, I can't see her face. I'm on the floor, but I hear her telling the one who had it in for me in particular to go and deliver a letter. She hands it to him. So this man goes off, the others go away. The woman says, 'Quick, get away! Get away!' She goes one way, I go another. From when I woke up my leg has been hurting me. They hit me so hard. I was terribly scared, I thought I would die."

Technical and theoretical considerations

At this point I think a few theoretical considerations are called for.

In crushing its enemies, state-sponsored terrorism attempts to impede their humanization, the slow evolution of their affections, their being considered subjects or individuals, their belonging to life, or being an expression of their existence.

State-sponsored violence rips them from their cultural and human background, from their family, social and affective history, from the smell and colour of their land. They are torn from the humus that for years has nourished them, from their roots which make them different and unique. They are rent from that area of absolute dependence on their environment which is ascribed at the deepest levels of human personality. "Our present ego-feeling", Freud writes in *Civilization and Its Discontents*, "is, therefore, only a shrunken residue of a much more inclusive—indeed, an all-embracing—feeling which corresponded to a more intimate bond between the ego and the world about it" (1929, p. 68).

The abuse of power tears them from the places where the first affective relationships, the primordial senses of self and basic belonging, formed by reciprocity and complementarity, are fashioned. This is the place where the undifferentiated, undetermined, and original nuclei of our existence are deposited; the place where ambiguity and symbiosis can find their way and leave their mark. The ambiguous and glutinous nucleus Bleger (1967) talks about in his book, *Symbiosis and Ambiguity*, is that which usually stays silent. The shadow is never dissipated and never asks to be inasmuch as it is understood and contained by the environment. In part, it is decanted in everyday gestures; in part it stays immobilized in the background, held up by the silent consensus of the community: a backdrop of security, the perfect synthesis and expression of its members.

The loss of this primordial relationship, in which one is indiscriminately and massively involved, is catastrophic. When this happens the "depository" is also lost and this is followed by an avalanche of further losses. The result is a cultural apocalypse, out of the ashes of which step the relentless and confusing ghosts of primary non-differentiation and initial persecution.

The fact that primary relationships, with the community and the family, have been cut off creates confusion, terror, and a sense of persecution. A state of extraneousness and the fear of not succeeding to survive takes over. Emptied out by the sudden cancellation of affective and social, inter-subjective, and trans-subjective identity, the ego is overwhelmed by a state of confusion. This can result in a longer- or shorter-term misting-over of the conscience and an invasive catastrophic anxiety, an experience of depersonalization and unreality, psychotic confusion and fragmentation.

Working with these patients it is important to remember that we are dealing with a spectacular failure of the social and the trans-subjective, the collapse of everything that had been taken as given. We are dealing with the mind's impotence, its inability to integrate, link, elaborate, or create associations for the affective/sensorial acceleration resulting from the brutality experienced. We are dealing with a profound sense of impotence, a total lack of defences, and an experience of disintegration and death.

These considerations mean that, for example, after the dream in which Carlo was being beaten, even though the role entrusted to me was explicit, I made the technical decision not to interpret this in terms of transference. I did not do this because the patient must be helped to distinguish the intense and sudden link that has been made between the primitive and undifferentiated areas of his mind, the glutinous nucleus, and the perverse violence of which he has been a victim.

In this dream, the patient has made a vital distinction. This is what must be stressed and reinforced, because he has to continue to pursue this path. At an intra-psychic level, there is a differentiation between good and bad people, between death and life. This same differentiation must be extended to distinguishing between his inner life and the state-sponsored violence whose "order", as Puget (1989) put it in the preface to his book, *State-Sponsored Violence and Psychoanalysis*, "… is not contained in the psychic space of the subject, but determines it without being able to recognise in it that which attains to his or her own personal violence" (pp. xvii–xix). Only then will the reality of events the patient lives in the present, be differentiated from those of his past.

The primary objective of this kind of therapy is to establish clear cuts, not to make whole a schizoid division.

Perversion is paramount in prison. Just as in the sewers all things are equal to their opposite, so between the prison walls there are false symmetries between the prisoner and the keeper, between the sequestered and the sequestrator. False equations make one similar to the other. Carlo has to free himself from all this; he has to go back to discriminating and differentiating between himself and the others.

It is up to me to help him in this process. His chance to pursue this path depends on my "non-ambiguity". To call myself in with an interpretation of transference will not help the patient. It may help him to shed light on the perverse fusion that he fears may have taken place between himself and his persecutors. Helping him to get away from the confusion in which he feels embroiled, to distinguish between himself and the others, means helping him to calm his profound states of confusion, his misting-over, and the shrinking of his conscience.

To abstain from interpretations of transference, a rule I always stick to, was even more necessary in this case. Carlo had escaped from prison thanks to the interventions of a woman, probably sent by his mother, who had succeeded in corrupting somebody in order to save his life. The dream he had helped us throw light on these figures and re-weave a dialogue with the interrupted past. Carlo's feelings towards his mother were strongly ambivalent. The fact that she was an intellectual and an adversary of the regime in power had unleashed the murderous wave that had washed over Carlo. Moreover, his mother was a woman involved in her work, who probably often left Carlo on his own. More crucially, she was absent, she had already been arrested when the soldiers broke into their house and dragged Carlo into prison.

The infraction triggered by these events, "… generates an alteration of the function and structure of memory that, so to say, freezes around the traumatic events and then irradiates its cone of shadow against the space or time preceding these events" (Sabatini Scalmati, 2000, p. 175). Therapy, by contrast, takes on the role and often the challenge of re-connecting the threads of the past, giving back life and keeping alive, even in moments of strong depression, the relationships with good objects, objects that we have to extract from the rubble, restore, and, fragment by fragment, bring back their colour and three-dimensionality.

It is in the order of terror to wipe out the space of the inner world, of subjectivity, of the circulation of affections and phantasmal representations. It is in the order of the therapeutic relationship to pay attention to the tiny fragments of memory concerning experiences and events before the patients' trauma. These fragments must be restored to life; the emotions and affections that once inhabited them must be given back, for these, unlike the traumatic events that succeeded them, made them feel alive and loved.

Back to the case history

Let us go back to the patient and his inner dialogue with his mother which slowly, we manage to reconstruct.

In one session Carlo succeeds in telling me, "Everything that has happened to me is terrible. These events have made me grow up in a hurry." The young man suffers but does not lay blame. He begins to remember a few features of his mother's character and those of other family members.

During the sessions communication is very intense; his emotions, anxieties, his feeling lost, images of terrifying episodes, the death of his prison mates, and the suicide of others. After about eight months, Carlo dares to rest his forearm on the edge of the table. This act of coming closer, of relaxation, his body no longer as contracted and his hands no longer clasped together, is accompanied by new difficulties and perse-cutory anxieties. "For me all is lost," he says, "I don't know what to do, how to live, and anyway I can't talk, I don't feel well."

Outside he works with commitment, he's doing important things, with good results. The medical tests he took excluded serious damage, but Carlo suffers from strong headaches and his nights are plagued by long hours of insomnia.

In one session he says, "I don't recognize myself in this body, I'm not happy in it. I grew up while I was in prison and … (silence) … I didn't want to tell you but I don't trust anybody, nobody."

His words lead me to dark, damp, and dirty places where sensations of disgust made his life seem nauseous, where his network of inner relations were constantly lacerated. Carlo grew up underground, his body has been humiliated, his penis charged with electric shocks. What effect will this have on his sex life?

Exposed to nudity and to his physiological needs, violated by the looks of others, deprived of the most basic conditions of hygiene and of any form of privacy, beaten and tortured, a human being becomes a body exposed to a terrible shame of itself. A process of dehumanization of this order soon cancels centuries of socialization and individuality.

His words give voice to a profound sense of solitude, to the distance in terms of space and time in which he lives most of his life, to a level of experience that, perhaps quite rightly, he feels I cannot understand.

Yet, while it is true that analysts' minds can only reach the psychic levels explored in their own analysis, it is also true that if their analysis and uninterrupted self-analysis have allowed them to hold at bay their own areas of ambiguity (Bleger, 1967), the misting-over of their own conscience, their own sneaky temptations to fall into the traps of the alienating and "pacifying" plots of institutions and power (Aulagnier, 1967), guided by their patients, without losing sight of their path, they can participate in the experience of horror about what mankind is capable of doing. To get close to the patients' experience and meet them at the place where the terrible split has taken place, a new sensation will make itself available to be invested with transference or counter-transference.

I reassure Carlo, telling him that what is at stake is not his trust in me or in other people near him, but his own ability and potential for sustaining himself on his own, for being able to hold together his self from the past and his self today, for facing up to his shame, because this shame stops him from taking care of himself completely.

His shame tells us about the internalization of other people's glances at him; their ridicule that has alienated him from his body, from his history and that today, alienates him from the community around him.

In prison, smell becomes humiliation and when your sense of privacy, of shame and then disgust, the veils that human beings wrap around themselves, are ripped away and trodden on, the mind shrinks away, looks away. Between the ego and the ideal of the ego, between the subject and the other subjects, a vast crater opens up. A passage from Freud's *The Ego and the Id* (1922) may help us give voice to the death fantasies that rise up in these moments.

> The fear of death in melancholia only admits of one explanation: that the ego gives itself up because it feels itself hated and persecuted by the super-ego, instead of loved. [...] The super-ego fulfils the same function of protecting and saving that was fulfilled in earlier days by the father and later by Providence or Destiny.

> But, when the ego finds itself in an excessive real danger which it
> believes itself unable to overcome by its own strength, it is bound
> to draw the same conclusion. It sees itself deserted by all protecting
> forces and lets itself die (p. 58).

Despite these oscillations, the defences that Carlo puts into play are
less violent; in addition to projection there is also introjection. Friends
become increasingly dear to him and his daily life takes on a lot of
changes. He is working and he is welcomed by a group of friends; he
starts to get closer to girls. He has some real concrete successes and
satisfactions. He succeeds in everything he does, although the price he
pays is a terrible struggle with himself.

When other people get too close to him, all his difficulties reappear.
Carlo perceives and suffers the differences. The comparison with "normality" is painful.

"If they get close it's worse. I can't manage," he says. On his face
there are new painful contractions, again a lump in his throat. The un-
sayable is suffocating him.

Comparison with his new friends has brought back to him, like a
mirror image, a warped image of himself, an orphan, different from
his perceived self. And yet he keeps on going. He wants to know what
happened to his parents, he starts to conduct research through the
Red Cross. He eats with difficulty. As always he wakes up before the
alarm rings, otherwise the sound terrifies him. Carlo still feels a pain
in his heart. "I thought," he tells me, "that things would change, but
when I'm with my friends I feel as though I'm in prison inside myself."
He gets angry with his parents who have not guaranteed him a life
like that of other young men, but at the same time he misses them
terribly.

His friends' houses stress this sense of nostalgia. We are going
through a difficult period. The fragility he seemed to have overcome is
always ready to come back.

The sessions go on. At times the mood is good; at others less good.
When he is more in touch with himself and can give voice to episodes
that weigh inside him, his suffering is more acute. A year has gone by
since our first meeting. One day he is particularly depressed, his face
tense. He says, "I'm only here in appearance, I can't feel my body. I'm
still there, it's stronger. I feel a lot of hate and anger and I always feel
I'm on my own."

Despite this, Carlo is better. His skin has taken on a healthier colour, more golden than the shades of green of the past. His life has opened up to new levels of experience. In everyday life he is doing well, he is part of a group. He likes his work and he enjoys seeing the people he goes around with. He even manages to laugh and have fun. However, at deeper levels, his traumatic experience continues to create a vacuum around him. After dinner at a friend's house, he has this dream, "I'm in a place, maybe a dinner, everyone's talking, but I feel I'm a stranger. I don't know what to say, I can't even understand what the others are saying."

We've been meeting for a year and a half when Carlo reveals something new as he comes into my room. He sits down and leans both his arms on the table, his body relaxed. His defence of immobilization seems to have been finally laid to rest. He says, "I dreamed I was in x (his country), with my friends and my girlfriend, before everything happened."

This "first time" allows him to talk about his father and his brothers, about his mother's affectionate and kind features. It allows him to recover affective links that seemed to have been broken, to distend his body, to lean on the table. Before leaving he says, "Now I feel more relaxed. I realize what it has done to me coming here; it has done me good."

Carlo is moving over an increasingly vast territory and the persecutory/depressive oscillations are less polarized. He is opening up to differentiated psychic qualities; he is struggling to build a network of relations. He is beginning to make plans for his future; projects he had begun to fantasize about in his early adolescence come back to mind.

In this period the possibility of suspending our sessions begins to be hinted at. One day he says to me, "I'll always have to reckon with what has happened, but now when I'm working I'm better, sometimes I even forget. This is the only place where I really feel in myself. Here I am whole. Maybe now even outside I'll be able to be less scared about what I feel inside."

There are still vast areas of fragility, but Carlo feels the call of new experience. I think I can let him go; for him the time has come to distance himself. We have given emotional expression and words to some of his terrifying experiences. Now he can begin to send away from his heart some of the images from his past.

Despite what he has seen and suffered, I think that Carlo will be able to deal with life and his own special existential suffering. We agree to meet until the summer holidays, obviously with the chance to start up again whenever he feels the need.

At the end of the final session, at the door he turns around, looks around the room and says, "In this place there are things that nobody knows about."

I have not seen Carlo since, but he has called me a few times. A few months ago he told me that he had decided to move to a city in the North where friends had found him a job.

CHAPTER FOUR

Internal homelessness

Paulina Reyes and Alejandro Reyes

Introduction

The need for new ideas about trauma is certainly arguable. Trauma is such a central concept to psychoanalysis; it is so much part of its very foundations that claiming new ideas about it may sound at worst pretentious, at best overambitious. Besides, so much has been written about extreme trauma and torture from every possible perspective within psychoanalysis or close to it, that the informed reader has the right to be sceptical about such claims.

Yet it is our belief that new perspectives are needed. Just at the moment when we are leaving behind the most violent century in history and just over a hundred years after Breuer and Freud's *Studies on Hysteria*, we are confronted with a situation where trauma suffuses everyday reality. We wonder if we are not reaching a point of social saturation making it legitimate to ask, has the irruption of the unexpected, the pathogenic, become the norm to the point of rendering the very concept of trauma meaningless? Or the converse of this idea; are we immersed in traumatized societies within which individual trauma needs to be made distinctive? As if in confirmation of such a context, a widespread eagerness to adopt the status of victim, a prevalence of individual and collective feelings of helplessness, a numbness in the presence of everyday horrors and, last but not least, states of emotional and cognitive ambiguity or un-definition, all of them characteristic attributes of the traumatized mind, are visibly gaining ground in society.

If this context is real, where can we offer a conceptual home to the victims of genuine man-made horror, such as those who have suffered persecution and torture? Shall we place them in an ambiguous atmosphere where their trauma is trivialized or diluted into a background of generalized social and historical trauma, where they would be ignored and left alone? Shall we confine their suffering within the same concepts of the developmental trauma we use to think of patients with borderline and narcissistic organizations, or within the comfortably reductive limits of a diagnostic category like PTSD?

It is our view that none of these alternatives does justice to the multidimensional nature of the loss and damage these people have suffered. We also hold the view that, at the turn of this century, the victim of torture or similar man-made horrors has taken the place that the hysterical patient occupied a hundred years ago, both in its potential as part of the growing edge of psychoanalysis as well as in the sense of the traumatized mind becoming a living testimony of its social and historical time. There is a need for an epistemology valid inside and outside the consulting room; valid for the internal world and for the external reality of therapists and patients.

We have used three categories in an attempt to obtain a wider view of trauma, trying to articulate them with the help of the ideas of Matte Blanco (1975, 1988) which are indispensable to this different perspective. These are the categories of: a) space, b) form, and c) exchange.

A. In the language of space

We believe that proper psychoanalytical understanding of the consequences of extreme man-made trauma cannot be achieved without a language able to give a coherent account of the destruction of the mind as an organization of differentiated spaces. These include the corporal, psychic, subjective, objective, and social spaces that feed, or used to feed, the mind of the traumatized patient.

The most general description of the destructive traumatic process in these terms would be as a nearly complete externalization of the person's internal world. This means that the person can "see" descriptions of their internal states only in displays of external situations and events. They are, in fact, forced to rely on these displays since they are unable to "feel" their experiences as their own, or to summon images of the experiences to their minds and "see" them as internal.

Such terrible loss of the subject, not comparable to any other mental pathology, including psychoses, results from the detachment of the thinking process from the corporal/emotional matrix that animates it. This is what patients can describe as feeling dead inside. In this state of mind the person not only has lost contact with an internal experience of their uniqueness, i.e., with an internal recognition of themselves as different from everyone else (in Matte Blanco's terms, with their heterogeneous or asymmetrical being), but have also lost contact with an internal experience of what they have in common with everyone else, their sense of continuity with the rest of humankind, their homogeneous or symmetrical being. In the first case, instead of uniqueness they experience isolation; in the second, instead of a sense of commonality of experience they have a feeling of dissolution of the sense of self.

In the victims' own descriptions of the horrors they have suffered and their aftermath, we have had a glimpse of the moment and manner in which these dislocations are produced.

Aided by spatial concepts, we have given the name of "internal homelessness" to the resulting traumatized organization, and described as "traumatized logic" the thought processes that express it which are characterized, in the main, by a restriction to categorical thinking (Reyes, Reyes & Skelton, 1997). This paper is a compilation of clinical evidence supporting and clarifying, we hope, each of the concepts we have outlined.

Matte Blanco (1988, pp. 70–81) proposes an understanding of the mind as the expression of our being in the world in two inseparable although incompatible modes: the indivisible or homogeneous and the divisible or heterogeneous. The first refers to our continuity or commonality with everything that exists, the second to consciousness of our discontinuity and difference, as well as of the infinite variety and diversity of the objects of experience. The two modes manifest themselves in thinking in two forms of logic that are the dialectical negation of each other; the "symmetrical" logic that seeks the equalization of all things, and the "asymmetrical", or Aristotelian or classical logic based on the rationality of contradiction and difference.

B. The category of form

The abstract nature of this theoretical model, which is based on the form of mental processes as opposed to their emotional contents or their meaning, enables it to describe in terms of thinking, the mind in all its aspects, from the deepest and most "mindless" aspects of the being, those encased in the body for instance, to the mind that has been totally externalized and has had its subject dissolved and lost in the social body. It is our view that the essential characteristic of the traumatized mind is the loss of contact with the subjective or internal side of emotional experience, with its contents and qualities, that is, with preservation of the forms these experiences might or should have. It can be said that these people preserve contact only with abstractions, or abstracted forms, of their experiences.

Thus a psychoanalytical theory like Matte Blanco's (1988, pp. 17–19), based on the form of processes, is able to complement the predominantly post-Kleinian view that guides our own observations helping us understand how the external, objective, and social spaces relate to the internal events that fundamentally shape the response to trauma. We call our use of Matte Blanco in this sense, a "psychoanalysis from the outside" which may be better placed to describe a mind increasingly alienated from its biological and social realities.

C. The exchange category

A third central concept we propose is the category of exchange, rarely used explicitly in psychoanalytical relationships, hence probably less familiar to the reader. Exchange is a category universal to all manifestations of life. It embraces the biological, economical, social, and intrapsychic domains. It implies movement between spaces that need to have qualitative differences, i.e., asymmetry, in order to sustain activity. Life cannot proceed without exchanges between different spaces, and psychic life is no exception.

An historical perspective

The ferocious political repression that gripped Latin America during the Sixties and Seventies involved some nations with fairly well developed psychological/psychoanalytical cultures. This made it possible to observe and document the impact of fear and acutely dehumanizing experiences on people and populations, in a manner that had not been available before. In the conceptual background stood the wealth of experience of the pioneering psychoanalysts who had treated the survivors of the Holocaust.

Critical analysis of these experiences, particularly those happening in Chile and Argentina, convinced us of the need to conceptualize, in psychoanalytical terms, all sorts of spaces, historical and political, subjective and objective, as intrinsic to the therapy (Lira & Weinstein, 1984). It was clear, for example, that the use of international arenas and tribunals, vast spaces where the injustices suffered by the victims were denounced, could be understood from a psychoanalytical perspective as indispensable projective/introjective processes and parts of the container of the therapeutic process. In certain instances, therapist and patient had to belong to the same "space of goodness", such as therapists working under the fragile protection of the Catholic Church during the dictatorship in Chile, for the patient to be able to separate goodness and badness, or defuse life and death instincts inside themselves, and project the badness out and away from themselves into a "space of badness". Likewise, a patient's need to travel in the company of others in order to prevent choking anxiety could be understood as a need for the space of projection represented by the two companions. More generally, the classically described "loss of basic trust" could be translated into an asphyxiating loss or lack of space for projective identification, a disturbance central to the traumatized state (Reyes, 1989).

Clinical observations

The following clinical example was decisive in expanding our understanding of trauma and gave us an entirely new perspective on the notion of substitute objects. It also made evident a process of exchange and its form.

Angelina and her four-year-old boy Damian, not their real names, were the only survivors of a young African family and had seen their husband/father and daughter/little sister killed in their presence. They had survived prison and threats of death and eventually found refuge in England without yet showing overt signs of disturbance. It had been the tragic, presumably accidental death of Angelina's twin brother, their only relative in England, which had precipitated mother and child into a severe post-traumatic syndrome state.

When they came to us, both showed the frozen state classically described for Holocaust survivors. Their affect was visibly flat, they were unable to feel, to cry, or to talk about the horrible traumas they had endured, unable to enjoy or laugh and Angelina said she felt "half dead inside". Mother and child had been equalized, symmetrized in Matte Blanco's (1988, pp. 17–19) terms, in emotional deadness; they could not talk to each other about their experiences and no emotional exchange seemed possible between them.

Yet the mother had found a bizarre way of creating an emotional gradient or differential between them and purposefully showed it to us: bending towards the child, her face very close to his, she said repeatedly "I'm going to die, Damian, I'm going to die" until the child broke down in tears, at which moment she embraced and comforted him.

With this apparently cruel manoeuvre, Angelina could manage to re-establish herself formally in a maternal function. The interaction involved: a) an enactment of the form, i.e., a dramatization of emotional exchange because, although the mother was not in touch with her emotions, she had preserved the abstract form of an emotional exchange; b) she had devised an interaction that was isomorphic with it; c) she had had to appeal to quantity to compensate for a difference, i.e., an asymmetry in quality that had been lost between them. The possibility of a bigger disaster had been introduced to intensify the distress in the child above breaking point thus allowing her to receive it. In order to do this she had had to place herself and the child on the same axis, on a linear arrangement in which differences could only be expressed in terms of being more or less, bigger or smaller. She had re-established a differential by creating a situation where she was bigger than her son, or his distress was bigger that hers.

Through the attempt at overcoming the failure of a process, this interaction managed to make evident its shape which would not have been available if the process had not been impeded. As Freud (1895d) often said, the distortion of the function enabled us to see its normality.

The behaviour we describe next does the same for the disarticulation of mental spaces with the loss of distinction between internal and external spaces.

The need to escape from an internal state

When Angelina was alone in her room the constant re-run of traumatic memories in her mind would become so intolerable that she had to open the door to hear the "noises of life" coming from the outside.

Thus the opening of the door can be seen as an attempt to escape a deadly internal state, seeking life from the outside. It can also be seen as signalling the dissolution of the boundary between internal and external spaces, and/or the inability to sustain an internal space.

At this stage we have to describe other aspects of Angelina's amazing mental state.

The symmetrization of the mind

Angelina was unable to be alone and so had to go out in company. She suffered a constant re-run of memories; her sleep was disturbed and she experienced recurrent nightmares.

On one occasion she arrived two hours early for her session. On another she telephoned, flustered, to apologize for not attending a session that had not yet happened. On yet another occasion, she arrived half an hour early but with the conviction that the session had already happened. This suggested a disturbance in the sequential experience of time.

She could talk about her twin brother as if he was alive and dead at the same time. She would say, for instance, that she had looked in the mirror and instead of herself she had seen her brother, a sure sign that he was alive. She would then talk about what she would say to him next time she saw him. In another session she told us how she was planning to make a biographical video of her brother using her son as the brother when a child. Because of her ambiguous talk, it was not clear at times if she was talking about her son or about her brother.

Thus she seemed to be living simultaneously in two incompatible realities: one in which her relatives were still alive, another in which they were dead. The distinction between past, present, and future seemed to have become blurred, in keeping with her disturbance in the sequencing of events in time. As in dreams, Aristotelian logic was simultaneously respected and not respected.

The logic of classes and the substitute object

As she was unable to leave home without company and not wishing to bring her own child, she had surprised us by arriving accompanied by a pair of black twin children, a boy and girl, whom she had "borrowed" from her neighbour. It seemed that the presence of these twins had enabled her to talk about her twin brother and their childhood together and to muster some measure of emotion. She had said of the little girl twin: "She is my little girl to me." To the next session she brought only this child, her physical presence ostensibly enabling Angelina to talk about the horror of witnessing the murder of her little girl and to express some emotion about it.

We realized that it was not any affective content of Angelina's relation with these children whom she hardly knew, but merely their external formal attributes, that enabled her to have some access, from the outside as it were, to an experience she could not access emotionally from the inside. This detour towards a visible form in external reality allowed her to have a mediated, self limiting access to the terrible experience of her daughter being killed in front of her. Real emotional exchange, either within herself or with us, was not obtained though, because at the moment of the emergence of the emotions, the whole experience was "projected" onto a screen becoming rather like crying when watching a film. The subject and the experience parted company, the experience remaining external as if happening to someone else.

The abolition of the boundaries between internal and external realities, that she had described in the opening of the door, had resulted in the enactment of the unconscious logic of primary process, or the symmetrical logic of Matte Blanco (1988, p. 19), where negation and contradiction do not exist. It coexisted without conflict in her thoughts and actions, with Aristotelian logic, as if she was in a dream state.

In conventional object relations terms, one can describe Angelina as using her neighbour's children as part objects. A Matte Blanco (1988, p. 78) perspective enables us to see that she had made use of attributes abstracted from these children, for instance from her dead child and from the "borrowed" one, she had abstracted (i.e., selected) skin colour, gender, and age to place both girls in the same class of "black girls aged two" and substitute the class for the individual. She was making unconscious use of a logical property of the class: since all members of a class have been equalized under the selected attributes that define the class, they have become symmetrically exchangeable.

It is the overwhelming nature of the feelings, in this case horror and probably guilt, that blows up the boundaries of the self/ego and their capacity to sustain the specificity or uniqueness of a relation. The feelings pertaining to this object relation can then find lodging and transport only in the massive, infinitizing form of the class, where they become diluted alongside the fragmented bits of self and object. In the symmetrical logic of classes, there is no difference between the individual and the class, hence the uniqueness of her object was certainly lost for Angelina but, with the help of objects of the same class, she could create an illusion of the continuing existence of her daughter and secure for herself a "continuity of being" in Winnicottian (1990) terms.

Here we wish to emphasize that:

a. The opening of the door that marks the dissolution of the boundary between internal and external reality, marks also the dissolution of the mind as a multidimensional arrangement of differentiated spaces, such as the disappearance of the memory as a compartment, or of the ego as a central agency or the superego as supervisory agency; the individual as a subject is no longer.

b. A multidimensional mind is reduced to a linear structure open to infinity. This is manifest in the substitution of the class for the individual. The class as a linear ordination of all objects with one or more formal attributes in common, is potentially an infinite series and cuts across the boundaries of the self.

c. The crucial role of abstracting visible, formal attributes of experiences and objects which is essential to the processes of externalization, formation of classes, and formation of substitute or exchange objects. The abstracted forms act as a sort of "scaffolding" in the reconstruction of a destroyed object relation.

d. The classes can be considered as containers of limited capabilities. Unlike containers providing alpha functions (Bion, 1963), they have no transformational powers since within a class there can be no change, only interchange of like with like; but they can act as carriers of object relations or fragments of them, from this point of view acting as a sort of memory. In turn, the formal attributes that generated the class fulfil a similar function to the headings in a filing system, enabling the "tracking" or recognition of the bits of self or object the traumatized person cannot afford to lose. In our view, the externalized classes are identical with Bion's beta elements (Reyes, Reyes & Skelton, 1997).

In the next clinical example we can see some of these psychic disasters in terms of the movement of internal object relations.

Torture and the language of space: the case of Laura

A. The need of a vast space to project herself far away

The clinical case that follows could not be meaningfully described without recourse to notions of space even at their most concrete levels. Laura, not her real name, a young woman with a history of imprisonment and torture in her native Latin American country, had been referred by a university in a northern city quite distant from London, where she was pursuing post-graduate studies, as there were serious doubts that she would be able to continue with them. She was suffering from insomnia, nightmares, inability to concentrate, and a peculiar difficulty in putting pen to paper. She was in a constant state of gloom and misery, and could not do any work in her own flat which she felt as a dark, barren territory that provoked in her intolerable claustrophobia. As in the case of Angelina, there had been a latency period of about a year in which she had remained apparently asymptomatic; it was when her dear brother who had come to stay with her in England left that she had broken down.

There was a specific plea for us to see her since we could provide therapy in her own maternal language and, being experienced in working with victims of torture, we were in a unique position to help, the tone of the referral somehow making us feel important and unique. Correspondingly, we devised for her an ad hoc form of therapy consisting of monthly sessions of one and a half hours' duration, with a male and female therapist in the room, in a homely setting which included coffee and biscuits. The sessions would take place on Saturday mornings and were free of charge.

At the time we thought we had very clear reasons to justify this modality of work, an important one being the fact that she had to travel a long distance to London to have her therapy. But it was not long before we became aware that ours was just part of a countertransference involving a considerable number of others that Laura had the capacity to cast or "radiate" over long distances. This represented her need, as we show later, to gather together object relations that had been exploded and dispersed over vast externalized psychic distances during her experience of torture. She could thus mobilize many people into creating situations of exception[1] and treat her as a unique person

---

[1] During her first years of therapy, with the help of influential people in her professional field, Laura had travelled to different parts of the world representing her British professional body. At the time this was well beyond her capabilities and seniority.

for whom exceptional and unique things had to be done, the power of her omnipotence being one of the most striking aspects of her case. Our own needs and omnipotence, as well as those of other people, were also involved, but early in the therapy we became aware that in her unconscious script we had been assigned the role of a parental couple that she as an exceptional daughter, had the task of bringing together and making creative.

B. Internal homelessness: a nearly complete externalization of the internal world

To the difficulty in staying, studying, or doing work in her flat, Laura added other experiences. She felt that this flat was so dark that her plants could not blossom in it. In consequence, she kept the plants outside in the communal space of the corridor, from where they were stolen leaving her in despair. As in the previous case, we were led to think that she felt dislodged from a central part of her being that had become uninhabitable, and felt the need to get away from it since it was a place made barren, persecutory, and inaccessible to thinking. Furthermore, there seemed to be an ongoing process through which she was depleted of vital aspects of herself.

During the first three years of therapy, Laura used to flood the sessions with stories of murders, massacres, or disasters, sometimes told in lurid, sadistic detail. These episodes, whether recent or distant in her past, whether related to her own personal history or apparently unrelated, such as events that were currently in the news, were all equally capable of unleashing in her a great deal of distress and provided an opportunity to cry abundantly in every session. After such episodes she seemed to be left in an exhausted and empty state which more than once she described as "being left at zero".

These gruesome accounts seemed to fulfil various functions. On the one hand, they seemed to be evacuations of mental states that left her depleted. On the other, they seemed to be elements of a process of exchange, a sort of currency with which she would excite our interest and probably keep us longing for more, this with slightly perverse undertones.[2]

But it also could be thought that these events which had in common their gruesome, disastrous nature, were an attempt at approaching,

---

[2]The experience reminded us of Anna O's "chimney sweeping" as described by Freud and Breuer in *Studies on Hysteria*.

from the outside as it were, an internal disaster that she could not directly express in a specific form as her own experience. That is to say, in order to be thought, these experiences had to be deployed and displayed as objects in the external reality.

Events that had the same emotional immediacy for her, whether they related to her or to other people, whether they belonged to a remote past or the present, suggested that for Laura, the differences between internal and external spaces as well as between past and present had been blurred.

That spatial distances also seemed to have been abolished in her mind is suggested by the following material. She told us that her partner, much against her wishes, is watching a television programme where hostages who had been recently freed in Beirut were being interviewed; she feels their voices persecuting her in every room in her flat she tries to escape to. Eventually she locks herself in the bathroom but the voices reached her there with the same implacable intensity.

We see now the similarities with the case of Angelina: to the abolition of distances in time and space, we can add a need to escape an internal space that has been rendered uninhabitable by the trauma; the need of a detour to the external reality and use of objects of similar formal attributes, i.e., of the same class as the objects that have been lost as in the case of Angelina, or of the same class of disastrous events as the one that had taken place inside herself, as in the case of Laura, in order to approach an internal experience that could not be given form from within and expressed. This process we have called "scaffolding" as it externally describes the form and site of the destroyed object relation.

The reader may have noticed a certain transparency in Laura's accounts, in the sense that everything she said seemed to be clearly describing internal states or events. Her mind felt like a thin film spread over the narrative of the objective events she was describing. The distance between the objects used as metaphors and the objects represented was so slight that on many occasions we were tempted into interpreting their meaning and thinking that what was obvious to us, should be easily made obvious to her. We sometimes shared the illusion that she gained insight from them. In retrospect, we think that Laura was a clear case of the total loss of authorship of her own thoughts. This has been described elsewhere for some survivors of the Holocaust who had to rely on the accounts of others to describe their own experiences (Niederland, 1967, 1981; Grubrich-Simitis, 1981). Thus, in her case, she could "see" and perhaps understand while with us but once she was away, all insight disappeared.

This process of loss of the subject is exemplified by a political anecdote she told us: "It was the 500th anniversary of the discovery of America and to commemorate the event, the Dominican Republic had built a gigantic lighthouse able to cast a light far into the Caribbean, but every time it was switched on, it drained so much electricity that it left Santo Domingo, the capital city, in a complete blackout."

This anecdote illustrates what could be surmised from her history and actions: how her call for help had taken the form of casting herself into vast distances as had been suggested by the modality of referral and subsequent happenings; how this was grandiosely experienced by her as if she was illuminating others at the expense and depletion of her own being, leaving her in a dark, barren territory. This had already been suggested by her account of her dark flat and the disappearance of her plants.

A memory from early childhood, probably a screen memory, revealed links between her present state of mind and her developmental history. Her mother would put her to bed at night, switching off the light and closing the door, ignoring the desperate cries of the child, terrified of the dark. Her father, on arriving home, would then walk in, switch the light on and comfort her by telling her stories.

The dark/light dissociation of her experiences suggests a structural link with dissociation in her internal parental couple. She was the youngest of five children and apparently her father's favourite, while her mother had used her as confidante to empty out her resentment against her husband, a womanizer, who had not protected the girl from involvement in his relations with other women. Both parents had informed an adolescent Laura that they would separate as soon as she left home and this had effectively happened when she prematurely left at age 17, to join the guerrilla movement active in her country.

Laura's experiences and discourse were permanently and universally pervaded by dualities that were at best incompatible, at worst mutually destructive. As with the case of the gruesome stories, we felt that this was her way of describing a radical, insoluble dissociation in her own self. Her own native colours were incompatible with the colours of British culture, the geography and climate of her country incompatible with Western architecture of steel and glass. The Spanish conquistadors had exploited and murdered the natives and Europeans had only come to the

Americas to exploit and massacre the Indians. White oppressors versus black oppressed; useless scientific medicine versus the effectiveness of native remedies, this and much more of a similar nature. The inability to put pen to paper was but one manifestation of this dissociation that we understood as a fantasy about the parents that she was unable to bring together. It could also be interpreted that her parents were universally represented in the form of these antagonistic classes in which her mother was, as a rule, on the side of the natives and the oppressed.

The vicissitudes of the parental objects during torture

In the third year of therapy Laura gave us a first account of what had happened during torture. It took the form of a dramatization, an "as if" account using Ariel Dorfman's play *Death and the Maiden*, which she had just seen. Through identification with the female protagonist in the play and the female therapist in the room, both of the same name and nationality, she identified with a class of women that she perceived as "looking well" and "being intact" regardless of any ordeals they may have suffered. This visible need of a physical representation of an intact woman, an intact external object, is similar to Angelina's need of the borrowed black girl aged two, to enable a dramatized reconstruction of an unbearable experience to take place.

A second account happened a year later and had strong sexual characteristics; in fact it was unconsciously used by Laura to allow herself to become pregnant. In a series of drawings that she showed us, she represented herself naked and blindfolded, as she had been during her ordeal. In this enactment the therapists, identified with the torturers, were supposed to be excited by voyeuristic and sadistic impulses into attacking her helplessness. More psychic "depth" was involved in this account based on a sadistic intercourse fantasy which, we believe, was the necessary condition for her to open herself to us and to pregnancy. It was her way of giving us and gaining herself momentary access to a core part of herself, overcoming her "internal homelessness".[3]

---

[3] It was remarkable that at the time we had moved the setting to NHS premises as we were ourselves in transient accommodation while in the process of moving house. Thus we were technically "homeless" and this unconscious sexual invitation could be seen as a way of giving us lodgings inside herself. A few weeks after this session, she informed us of her pregnancy.

She could not take responsibility for the cruel form of this access, hence the passivity, whereas the blindfold implied, like the lighthouse before, that we could see but she could not see.

From these two accounts we derived a more or less accurate description of her object relations during torture.

On being imprisoned and in terrified anticipation of what was coming to her, she could not summon her mother's image to her mind; no matter how hard she tried she could not visualize her. Instead, she had in her mind the image of her two dead grandmothers, both dressed in severe black. We understand this as an attempt to protect the mother object which is "cushioned" inside a class of devitalized mother objects structured on the grandmothers.[4] The torturers had announced their function and intentions as "to tear to pieces the mothers of people like her", in Spanish *"partirles la madre"*. Here she says something that we found particularly striking: "God knows how many mothers I rescued by not informing on people." We understood this as an expression of a process of fragmentation and expulsion, far away from the torture room, of her own maternal object, onto the mothers of her comrades, another protective attempt. What is projected here is part of the self linked to that part of the maternal object that provides "light", the mother as witness and as mirror of her identity, enabling her to know what was happening to her. This is the mother as a visible, shared object in actual reality.

One aspect of her terror was that "she knew too much" because while in the guerrilla organization, she had always managed to be close to those in power and have access to more information than she should have. At an unconscious level, this was linked to her feeling of having had more access than she should have had to the sexuality of her parents.

Her wish "not to know" had then been intense. One form of protecting herself had been the fantasy that her father was there in the room acting as "her accomplice"; that he and she were joined together in

---

[4]The importance of grandmothers, whether imagined or even hallucinated has been reported without interpretation in Holocaust survivors. The importance of the evoked dead grandmothers in Laura's case, and of a live grandmother accompanying Angelina and Damian in the prisoners' camp, suggest to us an understanding in terms of the protection or recovery of the maternal object when there is a felt threat to it with the help of a process such as "scaffolding".

torturing the mother. It was not Laura then who was being tortured but her mother located in Laura's body.

Unlike the previous attempts aimed at protecting the mother object, this one was aimed at rescuing the self. It was dictated by the terror and the wish to evade an unbearable reality, and had probably found form in an infantile masturbatory fantasy of penetration of mother with father's help, the torturers taking the part of the father opening for her a sadistic access. This had prompted her to say that she felt she was forever locked up in the torture room. It was also the moment when her latent dissociation had become radical and definitive. In Meltzer's terms, it was the moment when she had become irreversibly trapped, "ad infinitum", in a maternal "claustrum" inside her own body (Meltzer, 1992).

Two opposite movements had then taken place, tearing her being apart through two experiences of her maternal object, as effectively as if she had been quartered. These two parts of the self/mother experience are incompatible in time, this distance dictating the need for re-presentation. That this psychic distance had been made infinite during the torture was expressed in the need to project herself far away, while the light continuously receded from her, another instance of "infinitization" supporting our idea of two experiences of self that are incompatible in time and can only be bridged by symbolic representation, by the work of a subject that in her was lost.

Part of her had regressed into a closed system, inside an object that could give her life but only at the expense of becoming itself depleted and dead, with no possibility of replenishment from outer sources.[5] We believe that in this process, the tortured person carries with her the withdrawal of all that she had unconsciously projected onto the social and political fabric of her previous environment (Bleger, 1976); a compressed load charged with death instinct.

The moment during the process of torture, when the radical disappearance of the mother object able to recognize her identity is affected, seems to be this: the torturers allowed her to go to the toilet.

---

[5] Not long before these observations, an event that can be seen as a paradigm of such a closed system took place in Armenia: a mother and her six-year-old daughter were rescued alive after being buried for ten days following an earthquake. The mother had kept the daughter alive by cutting her fingers and allowing the girl to suck her blood. Whenever the girl was hungry or thirsty she would say "More, mammy, more" and the mother would reopen the cuts and give her more.

She looked at herself in the mirror and did not recognize herself; her face was monstrously swollen and she feared she had lost one eye. She had the impulse to kill herself, broke a glass inadvertently left there and made two profound gashes in her arm. She felt an immediate sense of liberation and relief; a wish to live.

At this point she seemed to be describing the liberation of an infantile part entrapped within the mother that was effected through a reproduction of the destructive attack on the mother's body, similar to the torture and similar to the original masturbatory penetration, enacted in the gesture of cutting herself.

Suicidal elements were to accompany Laura's enactments of this entrapping process. She had first shown the form of this fantasy during her second account to us of the torture, when she drew herself naked and blindfolded, inviting a sadistic attack; a mental representation of her opening to pregnancy. This had been preceded by a period of intense and persistent suicidal thoughts.

Another enactment happened when she was going to resume her studies and took her child to a child-minder for the first time: a separation that was terribly difficult for her. She parked in front of the minder's house and accidentally locked herself out of the car leaving the child inside. She desperately thought that there was no other way of freeing her crying child than to break the car window at the risk of hurting him. Eventually, with help from a neighbour, she called the rescue services.

Another incident took place during her second pregnancy. She said that she was unable to think of the baby inside her; she just could not imagine him. This ability seemed to have been taken over instead by her now four-year-old son who was anxious, constantly preoccupied with what was inside his mother, and unable to sleep because of this. We suggested a family session to address the child's high level of anxiety. We said that if Laura were able to think about the new baby inside her, this would relieve her four-year-old of the responsibility. After the family session, Laura had a serious fall down the stairs and had to be taken to the hospital by ambulance. However, she was not seriously injured and the pregnancy proceeded normally. Afterwards she told us that following this dramatic episode, she was able to imagine her baby inside her without difficulty, confirming once more her fantasy that the only possible access to the inside of herself or of an object was through violent means.

The process of exchange and the importance of abstraction

Between her first and second pregnancies, we witnessed an amazing process that can only be described and thought of in terms of the concept of exchange.

After giving birth to her first child, Laura remained in amenorrhea for two years. She was seen by specialists, a gynaecologist and an endocrinologist. Eventually, they assessed that her "ovaries were closed" and she was diagnosed with premature menopause. She was 34 years old and this was a disappointing blow for the couple who very much wanted to have a second child.

We had reason to believe that this premature closure was somehow meant for us. Two months previously, we had mentioned the need to introduce payment[6] in order to give her all the advantages of a professional relationship, most importantly the right to be angry and critical of us. In response, she had had an explosion of anger and had spoken of how when she had been taken to the torture room, she had urinated and soiled herself, and how after her ordeal, she had been left empty and had no recourse but to "close all her holes" in order to "keep in one piece". She seemed to perceive us as people who, not content with what she had already given us, were asking for even more. In this, we probably were very close to her torturers in her mind.

So when she told us about the premature menopause, we saw it as an emotional closure that had become expressed in her body. We voiced the hypothesis that over these past few years, she had felt compelled to enter into a form of exchange with us and probably with others, as if she had to offer or reveal aspects of her emotional being that other people could keep private. This had led to an exhaustion of her resources, particularly maternal resources bequeathed by her mother, which in her body had a seat in the ovaries and the rest of the internal genitals. That was why it was important that money entered to mediate in the exchange with us, protecting her emotional being. We agreed on a low fee, commensurate with her student status that would become effective the following session.

---

[6]Until then we had seen her as part of a "no-fee" therapy programme but after some years we felt that payment would introduce a needed dimension to the therapy.

Six weeks after we gave her the first bill she telephoned to let us know in joyous tones that she had found out that she was pregnant. Her doctors had said it was close to a miracle.

Her pregnancy was uneventful apart from the fall we have described. After the birth of the baby she gave signs that something new had emerged in her thinking, something we might call a preoccupation with, or an urge for, an element in herself or an object, endowed with mobility and an ability to move through different contexts, preserving a stability of form or identity; an object with the transcendent properties of the abstraction. She expressed this in the name she gave to the new baby which she chose because it was written and pronounced the same in several languages, so that the child would have no difficulties when in different countries. In the same and subsequent sessions, she talked about her brother-in-law who had qualities of balance and equanimity that enabled him to endure unaffected, various difficult situations and who, thanks to having dual nationality, was able to travel safely in and out of their dangerous country.

However, at the same time, events in her family life seemed to be depicting a chaotic, destructive version of this aspiration or the failure of it. Laura humorously described to us what she called the "family's musical beds". At night the baby would start crying, refusing to remain in his bed and this would end up with all family members displaced from their respective places, rotating through different beds and bedrooms, the couple becoming displaced from their bed and separated from each other. The baby would end up sleeping in every bed and bedroom but his own, as if he were empowered to undo all the spaces in the home. We thought he was enacting Laura's fantasy of the liberation of the entrapped child at the expense of the destruction of the container; that he was carrying the projection of that part of herself probably entrapped within the "claustrum" during her development, which had become further imploded during torture. This explosive return of the "repressed" seemed also to reproduce her infantile wish to have access to all spaces without exception, as she had to her parents' sexuality and later to privileged information that was above her capabilities. Last but not least, it reproduced the dissolution of the mental compartments that had been among the first manifestations of her traumatized mind.

We thought of this as an enactment of a failure of symbolic representation, of the capacity that enables us to maintain a stable representation of self and object through different mental compartments. But we also thought it plausible that the introduction of money, the abstract instrument of exchange, as a mediator in our relationship had triggered something in Laura's mind. This something had presumably given her and us access to that secluded, exhausted maternal object in herself, and had led to the experience of pregnancy and birth. Although this was not in itself an actual capacity for abstract representation, it was at least a longing for it and a notion of its nature.

But there was another possibility not exclusive of the first. Like many victims of torture, Laura lived an internal, desolate loneliness that excluded her from the human world. The actual moment that feeling had set in during her ordeal was suggested by an experience she recounted. It was Easter. She could hear the toll of church bells and from the street the noises and voices of people going to Mass. The torturers had taken a break and she could hear them praying too. At that moment she had had an agonizing feeling of being forever doomed to be isolated from the ordinary human world by an insurmountable barrier that included these men, who themselves were part of this world whereas she was not.

Notice that in this particular account of Laura's, unlike all the others we have described before, no particular object relation seems to be involved; she is not attacking any objects, no objects are attacking her, nothing is being projected. She was simply excluded from the world and cast into an objectless nothingness. The only possible object relation, in the sense we understand them in psychoanalysis, was through a perverse, evil object that definitively barred her from the world of goodness.

Hence, we are justified in thinking that the contract with us allowed her to re-establish the "social bond" (Clerc, 2000) or to be included again in the "social synthesis" (Sohn-Rettel, 1984) of which money is a sign (Arnaud, 2003). This liberated her transference to us, opening other possibilities beyond being her torturers or the parents she had to bring together. This point seemed to mark also a general improvement in her relationship with the world that became visible in a continuing improvement in her quality of life, family relations, reconciliation with her parents and expressions of her artistic creativity that took place in the next two years or so.

Discussion

"Internal homelessness" is a poetic term to designate something terrible. Not having direct access to their own experience as uniquely theirs means that our patients access it only through what it has in common with the experience of others; they can only have an experience of the object in terms of what makes it comparable or equivalent to objects of similar external attributes. The subjective experience of the object is lost.

We have described how our patients have to use objects or events in external reality to prevent the total loss of their externalized psychic reality. This use is not new. Bion described a psychotic man's use of objects in the room in an attempt to approach thought (Bion, 1963, pp. 39–41). What is new is the evidence of an unconscious logic at work in the use of such objects; they are organized in classes or sets according to formal similarities with the objects that are felt lost or destroyed as internal. As such, they serve as containers of the unbearable experiences, albeit insufficient ones, in the sense that they allow the traumatized person to carry their undigested memories and experiences alongside the bits of self and object attached to them, in this external form. The formal attributes organizing the class, such as "little black girl aged two", would serve a function similar to the headings in a filing system, enabling the recognition of the object that is carried, cushioned, diluted, or hidden, according to need, inside the class. Elsewhere we have highlighted the similarity of Bion's description of beta elements as an "abortive prototype of a container" and "aspects of the personality linked by a sense of catastrophe" (Bion, 1963, pp. 39–41) with the elements externalized and organized in classes. Notice, for instance, Laura's repetitive accounts of events "all linked by a sense of disaster".

The need for traumatized patients to anchor themselves in the perception of a visible form of the object, in order to approach areas of experience threatened by formlessness and darkness, justifies our use of the concept of "scaffolding" to define an important function of "class thinking" in the reconstruction of an object relation.

The nature of the radical dissociation

Two particular categories seemed to be at play in the minds of both of our patients. We describe them as uniqueness and exchangeability. Uniqueness is a category rooted in the biologically specific links between mother and infant.

In Angelina, the uniqueness of the lost object, her daughter, is intolerable. This prompts her to turn her into an object of exchange with the help of symmetrical logic. The part of her mind where the uniqueness of the mother-child relationship should be is felt as dead and uninhabitable. This is close to a physical feeling.

Laura, on the contrary, is entrapped in dark, lifeless territory. She seeks light through a peculiar way of seeking recognition as unique by vast networks of people, the light constantly eluding her, always remaining on the side of the other. The dispersion of her uniqueness onto so many people, plus her striking internal relationship with the light and the dark, suggested that a split had taken place between two structural components of the self, two basic relations, self and object.

One would be the biologically rooted experience of being at one with the mother. This is a "blind" experience that is in itself incommunicable in direct terms; it can only be expressed indirectly in the form of comparisons, or in terms different from itself, that because of this can never provide a full account of it.[7] This process of continuous approximation that can never give a full account of something lies at the roots of the search for meaning. The incommunicable experience would be identical to the experience of being; however, in psychoanalytical terms, we cannot conceive of an experience that is not relational.

The biologically rooted experience of uniqueness is identical to the anticipation of total fit, the unique fit that can never be attained. It cannot really become experience without the contribution of another side of the self, the side given by the experience of otherness and difference, Matte Blanco's (1988) experience of asymmetry. It is with these two points that we build the unique angle from which we try to translate, never with complete success, from the blind self towards the social and the objective.

This is the angle that has been lost in Laura. To acquire meaning, things need to exist at two levels; for the person as object and for the person as subject. Of these, only one is accessible to her. That is why she cannot see her mother's face or imagine her baby inside. Laura can be an object in herself but she cannot be an object for herself.

It is the total fracture of these two parts of the self and of the object that effects the complete failure of symbolic representation and psychic

---

[7]The experience of uniqueness would entail the paradox of feeling simultaneously "at one" with the mother and separate (different) from her. In Matte Blanco's terms this would be experiencing the confluence of maximum symmetry ("the same as") and maximum asymmetry (yet "different from").

timelessness. This separates Laura's disturbance from a developmental disorder resulting in a borderline or narcissistic organization. Neither do we believe her search for uniqueness to be simply a narcissistic manifestation. Her transparency enables us to clearly see the developmental "endogenous trauma" (Britton, 2005) in her; but we can also clearly see the influence of the external traumatic event whose hallmarks would be the total dissociation of the self resulting from the dual process of implosion/explosion through which these two parts are lost to each other; the nearly total externalization of the subject, internal homelessness, and the experience of part of the self as dead.

It can be said that the terrible split we have observed alienates the person from their primary biological being or primary nature, leaving them only in contact with an abstract relation to reality, or relation to an abstracted reality, the so-called second nature, i.e., the mental attributes developed through the social experience of humanity, but not with her unique experience of the world as an individual. What we are proposing is a comprehensive clinical approach that would make possible a view of these two natures and their interrelation without abandoning a strictly psychoanalytical stance.

CHAPTER FIVE

The post-traumatic nightmare: the *via regia* to unconscious integration?[1]

Liselotte Grünbaum

This chapter deals with a specific type of difficulty in psychotherapeutic work with children and adolescents massively traumatized by repeated assaults experienced through war, organized violence, and torture. In a number of cases, psychotherapy will have to begin with the consideration that although the young person in question is driven into therapy by severe post-traumatic symptoms and is therefore motivated, all possibilities for a subjective dialogue seem to be blocked. Some of these young people seem to have retreated into a mainly non-verbal, frozen, and depressive state, which opens very few possibilities for a therapeutic process to develop, regardless of whether the focus is on inner or external reality, or on the past, present, or future. The result may be that the sessions are dominated by stereotypic complaints about symptoms, interrupted by long periods of heavy silence in which the therapist is unable to think. This problem is especially relevant when dealing with young people and

---

[1]Some the case material presented in this article was first presented at a Conference of the European Federation of Psychoanalytic Psychotherapy, (Rome, 1 to 3 October 1999) and earlier published (Grünbaum, 2000; 2001).

children who have passed the age where play can be used as a means of communication. The dead and paralyzing atmosphere may result in bringing the session to a deadly standstill, the inertia of which is hard to bear and difficult to break.

In my experience, the primary therapeutic difficulty when dealing with these children and young people is for the therapist to find a way in which to approach the terror-stricken, frozen state which I assume lies behind the silence, and bring it into the dialogue. In other words, the problem for the therapist is how to establish a bearable dialogue with the young person about the unbearable.

Silence as an expression of a trauma-related breakdown and fragmentation of the unconscious formation of symbols, and at the interpersonal level as an expression of an unconscious alliance to avoid consciousness and remembrance of extreme human cruelty, has been discussed by numerous writers since World War II, often under the name of "the conspiracy of silence" (see, for example, Adelman, 1995; Danieli, 1981, 1984; Krystal & Niederland, 1968; Krystal, 1971; Laub & Auerhahn, 1993). In this chapter I wish to take this view further and also look at methodology, especially the fact that post-traumatic nightmares often seem to be a useful key to approach the psychotherapeutic process.[2]

The chapter is divided into three main sections. The first section is a theoretical examination of adolescence as seen against the background of a young refugee's integration of massively traumatizing experiences from earlier periods of his life. The next section is a theoretical discussion about the rudimentary symbols and psychodynamic functions of the post-traumatic nightmare. My hypothesis is that despite the repetitive, factual nature of these dreams, they often hold some sort of beginning of symbolic dream thoughts which, if contained and interpreted in the here and now of the transference relationship, in time may develop further and strengthen the reparation of the ability for unconscious symbol formation and linking with phantasy of good inner objects. In the final section, to illustrate my thoughts, I present clinical material from the treatment of a young man of 15 years.

---

[2]In accordance with Lansky et al. (1995), the post-traumatic nightmare is defined as a frequently recurring nightmare, during which the psyche in a factual and stereotypic way replays certain aspects of a specific traumatizing chain of events.

Adolescence: a second chance to integrate trauma

By adolescence I mean the period of time from the beginning of puberty to early adulthood, however this is defined in any given culture. During this period, a young person is expected to acquire the basic knowledge and skills necessary to cope as an adult in the culture to which he or she belongs. While the beginning of this period is determined by biological criteria, the end is culture-specific. Adolescence can thus, as suggested by Castillo (1996), be understood as a bio-culturally defined, universal period of passage during which the young person acquires and practises these specific skills and rituals, which both concretely and symbolically mark their existential death as a child and rebirth as an adult with the right and ability to get married and have children.

In industrialized societies like Denmark, with complex educational and occupational demands, young people are seen as adults later than in pre-modern societies, such as those which comprise many of the countries from which Denmark receives refugees. Consequently, the period of adolescence is longer in Denmark, stretching far into the age at which the young person is, in a biological sense, capable of functioning as an adult. In pre-modern societies, the period is shorter and the rituals more explicit, the young person having usually already learned at an early age the practical skills he or she requires to function as an adult.

The period of youth, as described by Blos (1989), can be seen as a period in which the young person faces, among other things, developmental tasks related to the integration of the unconscious residues of earlier trauma as well as the consolidation of a sense of personal historical continuity, meaning, and integrity, thus giving these aspects of personality development a second chance. This development takes place within a wider psychological context in which the increased demands both of psycho-biological potential and of social obligations, such as those relating to education and/or the obligation to contribute towards maintaining the family, will bring the acquisition of independent competence and function into focus. In this period of life, the young person to some extent gradually has to give up the legitimate right of the child to use his parents as a protective extension of his own self. This process brings in its wake an irregular state of flux between regressive and progressive movements, probably especially so in the prolonged adolescence of modern Western society. The young person briefly touches on infantile wishes, feelings, and ways of functioning otherwise left behind, the result of which seems to be that the now more mature self of the adolescent is faced anew with certain aspects of the inner child, such as subjective traces of earlier trauma. As a consequence, these regressive fluctuations inherent in adolescent development may offer the self a new opportunity to work through earlier trauma at a more mature level.

Obviously, to massively traumatized young refugees, this development may be especially difficult and may cause temporary reactivation of fundamental paralysis, terror, and anxiety of survival. Herein lies a developmental risk but, seen from a therapeutic point of view, also a possibility for a new and better integration of the anxiety-ridden traces of the past. Moreover, it seems clear that the subjective establishment of a continuous and meaningful personal history may be inhibited not only by the young person's own, understandable wish to avoid painful memories of trauma and loss, but also by the above-mentioned unconscious vow of silence between the members of the family (Adelman, 1995; Danieli, 1981).

Looking at these problems from the perspective of a theory of separation-individuation, Blos (1989), with reference to Mahler et al. (1975), refers to the period of youth as the second individuation process, defined as a process of inner separation-individuation in relation to infantile ties, the result of which is that the young person moves towards a more fully delimited personal identity and an inner freedom to make their own choices.

However, this understanding of the separation-individuation process as fundamental to the development of the adolescent self is based on a view of human nature that favours individualism, and in which the autonomous, self-sufficient individual, to some degree, is idealized. The ego-ideal of psychoanalysis may, to some extent, be said to be a person with a relatively firm differentiation between the inner and the external world, that is, between the subject's own and other people's feelings, thoughts, and fantasy. As suggested by Roland (1996), in that respect, psychoanalysis more than any other psychological theory may be understood as a product of the Western culture group, and it may be questioned whether this view of human nature is transferable to cultures in which the autonomous individual is not seen as the desirable aim of development. It is outside the scope of this chapter to discuss this complex issue further, because it would lead to a discussion of how to understand the psychoanalytic concepts of the unconscious in a cross-cultural context (Grünbaum, 2005, 2007; Roland, 1996).

In the following, I assume that from a cross-cultural perspective, it makes sense to understand adolescence as a developmental period in which a universal polarity or dialectic between the dimensions of separateness-interdependency finds a subjective synthesis in which cultural, familial, and personal features are contained.[3] This development is assumed to usher in another developmental need of the adolescent, namely the need to reintegrate and revise the family myths internalized during early childhood, so that these may be experienced from an adult rather than an infantile perspective. Consequently, a young refugee with family roots in a primarily collectivist culture group, but living their everyday life in an industrialized northern European country such as Denmark, will inevitably experience both interpersonal and intrapsychic conflicts relating to a bicultural identity.

The young person is thus faced with a dual psychological and social task of reconciling the different aspects of the self. On the one hand, there are the unconscious aspects of what Roland (1996) called a traditional "we-orientated self", the outer boundaries of which are inclusive in the sense that the differentiation between self and object allows a certain degree of fusion with a limited number of inner object representations established in infancy and early childhood, as an inner structure, and in the present, supported by social expectations from parents and other important members of a primary affiliation group. On the other hand are the likewise unconscious, as well as conscious aspects of object relations, introjected in later childhood, in a Western sense, an "I-orientated self", which in the present is supported by friends, schools, and social workers, since all expect that the young person has the right and duty to make their own decisions concerning, for example, education and financial matters as well as friendships and love relationships.

In this context, conflicts relating to the bicultural identity of the young person must be expected to strengthen the developmental need to make a critical re-evaluation of the past, including a re-evaluation of both their own and their parents' role in earlier, traumatizing events. It is thus likely that the by now increased capacity of the young

---

[3]I owe the dimensions separateness-interdependency to Blass and Blatt (1992).

person to develop independent views of the family history may lead to an intense inner conflict and, consequently, to feelings of guilt and shame.

The post-traumatic nightmare: a road to containment of traumatic disintegration?

For children, adolescents, and adults alike, dyssomnia with repetitive nightmares is a commonly described consequence of trauma (Terr, 1991). These nightmares, which may be repeated in a more or less identical fashion, usually contain specific fragments of memories from actual events which led to, or occurred simultaneously with, the traumatic reaction. Post-traumatic nightmares are followed by intense anxiety; the child or young person can describe waking up in an unclear state of mind where he or she believes they have gone back to the time and place of the nightmarish events, previously experienced in a waking state. Post-traumatic nightmares pose a recurring, painful reminder of the trauma and may be expected to maintain the post-traumatic symptoms.

Especially with regard to young people, this kind of post-traumatic blocking of the ability to produce normal, developmental dreams is likely to contribute to difficulties in handling the developmental tasks of the adolescent period. Ladame (1995) has suggested that during this period, an especially close connection exists between the ability to dream and the possibility of constructive, outward actions. At this age, psychosexual pressure combined with the regressive tendencies of puberty put the young person's capacity for self-regulation to the test, one result of which is an increased risk of impulsive behaviour. Ladame suggests that the capacity to dream to some extent neutralizes this pressure, as disturbing impressions and impulses from the dream are converted into symbols and at the same time given a certain means of expression. In the psychotherapeutic process, the question soon presents itself of how the therapist may best respond to the young person's complaints about these nightmares and, if it is possible through interpretation, to remove the blocks to dream developmental dreams.

In often-quoted words, Freud (1929) described the interpretation of dreams as the via regia to knowledge of the unconscious element in our psychic life (1960, p. 474). However, he excluded post-traumatic nightmares from this understanding because of their concrete repetition of unprocessed sense impressions, such as visual impressions of the traumatizing chain of events. The images of the post-traumatic dream are not as such derived from symbolic thinking related to unconscious fantasy, but should perhaps rather be looked upon as a mere abreaction of the traumatic overload of the psyche (Freud, 1917). The following years brought an increased understanding of the capacities of the ego for defence and mastering, in the light of which this originally very simple model was elaborated. In time, the tendency of the psyche to repeat overwhelming, traumatic images came to be seen as a variation of the tendency to identify with the aggressor. It was seen, that is, as the delayed attempt of the psyche, through repetition, to turn passive into active and thus master the traumatic flood (Freud, 1920; A. Freud, 1936). Since then, this view seems largely to have prevailed across psychoanalytical schools, without further adjustment (Young & Gibb, 1998; Srinath, 1998).

Exceptions to this are Lansky et al. (1995) and van der Veer (1993), in whose works the focus is on the therapeutic possibilities contained in the factual repetitions of the nightmare. Lansky et al. made a detailed analysis of psychotherapeutic sequences with American Vietnam veterans, concluding that post-traumatic nightmares, despite their non-symbolic form, may be understood along the same lines as other dreams, that is, as over-determined communication concerning unconscious but currently dynamic problem areas. They thus hold that the post-traumatic nightmare is shaped against the background of a combination of current impressions, memories of traumatizing sense impressions, and symbolic dream thoughts. In a psychotherapeutic process, this entails the post-traumatic nightmare, like any other dream, being understood as the product of a present context consisting of the external everyday life of the young person and the here-and-now transference relationship, as well as the present unconscious situation, in which anxiety, needs, wishes, and conflicts are actualized.

Some remarks concerning the application of the clinical case

Before I embark on the clinical case, I want to add a few words on the merits and problems connected with a psychoanalytic case study such as this. A thorough discussion of the pros and cons for using the psychotherapeutic process as a method for the collection of scientific data is outside the scope of this article. However, leaning on a hermeneutic perspective, psychoanalytic psychotherapy with children and adolescents can be considered a unique possibility for the study of data that presupposes the creation of a specific therapeutic setting, as well as a specific relationship and dialogue between child and therapist. The presented case study is based on a qualitative analysis of my recorded notes (below named "process notes"), as these were written down immediately after each single therapy session. This method of data collection of course has its limitations. For instance, the collected body of data is dependent on my subjective memory, even though I made an effort to remember all details. Furthermore, the process notes from even a relatively short, non-intensive therapy like this, when collected, make up quite extensive material. This holds numerous possibilities for selection and interpretation. While I have read and pondered on the entire collection of process notes more than once, the presented selection is focused only on such parts of the material that concern the problems I wish to explore. Consequently, many aspects of the therapeutic dialogue and process have been left out. In the following, I attempt to clarify my systematization of what is in fact subjective by relating the qualitative analysis to theoretical concepts. I have distinguished between direct quotations from the process notes (by indentation) and my subsequent thinking about this (appearing in plain text). The subjectivity of the therapist's own conception of the therapy is triangulated somewhat by adding information from the external reports from parents and teachers, evaluating the boy at the time of referral and at the end of treatment. Hopefully, my selection of parts of the case data and the interpretation of these to the reader will impart a proper disciplined subjectivity. Finally, one may ask why the work of a single therapist with a single young person is at all of a broader interest. I hope that my reflections on the therapy with this troubled young man may be useful to other therapists in their own work with traumatized children and adolescents.

A clinical case: Mohammad[4]

At 15 years of age, Mohammad was referred to psychotherapy by his parents, who described his anxiety, depression, sudden outbursts of

---

[4]For reasons of anonymity, a number of changes have been made regarding the background information as well as a few, more specific details in the quoted process notes.

rage, and severe dyssomnia with nightmares during which, in his sleep, he screamed and lashed out in anxiety. His ability to concentrate was reduced, and he suffered from an almost complete inability to learn, as a result of which he was having difficulty, for example, learning Danish. His inability to learn was a cause of worry to both himself and his parents, and he sincerely wished to do better in school.

When he was 13, he had come to Denmark with both his parents and a sister who was six years younger than him. According to his parents, his early development had been without problems. They had always thought of him as an intelligent child. The family was well off, but had belonged over several generations to an ethnic minority group in their native country. The family circumstances were relatively secure until Mohammad reached the age of four to five years. From this time on and until the flight to Denmark, family life was marked by war and a growing ethnic persecution which, among the other trials they had to face, led to the family's recurrent need to flee and evacuate within the country. Mohammad's schooling and relations with peers thus lacked continuity, and his ability to move freely in the local community was restricted by his parents in an attempt to secure his safety. His father, who participated actively in the resistance against a brutal, authoritarian regime, was often away from home and at times imprisoned.

Among several potentially traumatizing events in Mohammad's childhood, one critical episode stands out which, according to his parents, changed him from being a happy, loving, and lively boy to being sullen, introverted, and anxious, suffering from nightmares and dyssomnia. They recounted that at the age of nine years, on his way home from school, Mohammad had been taken hostage by government soldiers with the purpose of forcing his father to turn himself in. Mohammad was detained for 24 hours and endured psychological torture in the form of humiliation, mental abuse, threats of execution, and threats to the life of his parents and sister. When the father consequently turned up at the police station in order to save his son, Mohammad was forced to witness the beatings and humiliations of his father; he was also told that he would never see him again. Afterwards, the father was imprisoned and severely tortured. In the following years, the mother and children were more or less on their own, although they received some support from the father's family. During this time, the father was mostly away from home, sometimes imprisoned, sometimes in a war, and sometimes hiding from the authorities. Meanwhile, government soldiers looking for the father and other male members of the family frequently searched the home of the family.

At the time of the referral for psychotherapy, the life of the family was marked by violent fights between the parents on top of the father's physical and mental damage from the torture, as a result of which he was sometimes mentally unstable and, amongst other things, liable to paranoid control of his son's movements outside the home.

The setting

The therapy was conducted on a weekly basis for just over a year, since throughout the process Mohammad rejected my suggestions of more frequent sessions. He also refused to have an interpreter, since both he and his parents considered it to be a safety risk. Mohammad received no other kind of support or treatment during this time, but the parents were in parallel treatment with other therapists. Together with the parents, I took care of all coordination and consultation with the school and the social worker. This transgression in my role as Mohammad's therapist was unavoidable due to the lack of other possibilities. I tried to avert the negative consequences of this by bringing Mohammad to the meetings with the school and the parents, but it may still have influenced the fact that he refused more frequent meetings as well as wishing to end the treatment as soon as his symptoms abated.

The psychotherapeutic process

In the initial phase of therapy, Mohammad was quite apathetic and withdrawn. However, he usually appeared for the agreed sessions, which he would always start by hiding his face in his hands, nothing more happening unless I took the initiative. At times, this ongoing passivity was interrupted by repetitive complaints about his parents, the teachers, and other adult authorities. In session after session, these complaints were put forward in a flat voice, devoid of feelings, repeating again and again exactly the same sentences. The content mostly concerned the present, but was interspersed with bitter remarks about the father's frequent absence from home during his childhood, including the fact that the political choices of the father had brought in their wake grave suffering for mother and children. Dialogues about the content of his statements tended to get stuck, as my comments apparently could not be taken in, but were dropped in mid-air between us. Apart from these repeated sentences, Mohammad flatly refused to talk about the past. He would occasionally touch on traumatic events, but these brief descriptions were quite confused and vague, although an unmistakable, recurring theme related to avoidance and flight. He directly expressed a wish to focus on the present and the future, but was unable to hold on to his interest in these areas. A coherent dialogue with Mohammad was thus rarely possible; he kept losing track, retreating into an empty silence apparently devoid of thoughts.

Against this background, conversation about his recurrent, painful nightmares slowly developed and turned out to offer good enough containment for a therapeutic process to develop. Mohammad's motivation for bringing out his nightmares was initially prompted more by a wish to get rid of painful feelings than by the need to think about and understand his experiences. Thus, for several months, he recounted one or more nightmares in almost every session. Initially, I did very little except to listen. Out of this developed a specific relationship in which Mohammad unburdened himself, thereafter becoming more lively and for some time able to talk more fluently about current, external reality, such as his conflicts with his parents, his inability to learn, and his educational wishes.

A theme of unending persecution and flight

Over the months, with few details, little variation, and no spontaneous associations, Mohammad kept repeating the same stereotypic dream scenario in which aspects of life-threatening, external reality was prominent. In these dreams the family together was trying to escape from government soldiers through the mountains of his native country, the same mountains in which he and his family had often stayed during flight or evacuation. These dreams appeared in two variants:

1. Mohammad and his family are fleeing on foot through the mountains, followed by soldiers. They are running, but the soldiers get closer and open fire. The whole family, including Mohammad himself, is shot, after which he wakes up screaming in terror.
2. Mohammad flees alone through the mountains, followed by soldiers. He is running, but they get closer and open fire. He is shot and wakes up in terror.

As mentioned, Mohammad was unable to reflect on his dreams, but recounted them with no other comment than, for example, "It's the same as last time." Afterwards he would stop, and if I tried to enter into a dialogue with him by asking, for instance, how he felt recounting these nightmares to me, he would usually just withdraw into silence. As mentioned, his mastery of Danish was not very good, and in these moments he would often claim that he did not understand what I was saying. In my counter-transference, I felt even more that my ability to think and feel disappeared, even to the degree that I experienced a kind of linguistic paralysis, unable to make myself understood. I also found myself trying to silence my own doubt as to whether I would be able to help him by taking the stand that, in this phase of the therapy, he needed more than anything someone just to listen and bear with him.

After almost four months, the session recorded below took place. Seen in retrospect, this session seems to have heralded a change, because the persecution-flight theme of the nightmare here, for the first time, contains an inversion of the relation persecutor-victim. Also, in this session, for the first time I felt a clear connection between the here-and-now of the transference and the context of the dream in the session:

> Mohammad starts the session by complaining about his father, who shouts at the rest of the family all the time, wants to be in charge of everything, is suspicious of Mohammad's friends and whereabouts, and also refuses to give him pocket money like everybody else. Mohammad goes on to talk about a school report he has just received. This was not up to his expectations; he keeps getting bad marks especially in Danish lessons, as his Danish teacher doesn't understand his difficulties in learning the Danish language. He then recounts the following dream:
>
> He is on the run through the mountains, pursued by a group of soldiers. He is very frightened. When he looks back, he spots his father among the soldiers, holding a machine gun. He wakes up in a muddled, terrorized state.

For the first time in the therapeutic process, it was now possible to discuss the persecution theme of the dream with Mohammad. Together we could understand the dream both in the light of his, at the present time, troubled relationship with his father, and in the light of the transference, that is as to whether I would be able to understand him, in comparison to the Danish teacher who did not.

Mohammad's introductory remarks on the present, external situation in the family were probably quite realistic. However, at the same time, in the dream he seemed unconsciously to consider the risks taken by entering into a relationship with the transferential object because at this level, his reference to the unsupportive, demanding Danish teacher may also be seen as a reference to linguistic problems of expression and understanding in the therapeutic process. It was probably no coincidence that a change in the manifest content of the dream occurred at the same time as Mohammad unconsciously seemed to view his relationship to the therapist from a new perspective. Moreover, this new development implied a symbolic and emotional investment concerning an actively attacking, rather than passively escaping fatherly object. His location of the father among the persecutors in the dream thus seemed to hold a dawning, unconscious processing of the fact that the father, due to his political choices, had in part been responsible for the traumatizing experiences of the family and Mohammad.

On the face of it, this may seem to signify a dangerous development, since the self in the dream was left entirely without allies, and the relation to a primary object was entirely dominated by intense survival anxiety. However, it turned out in the following sessions to the contrary; this change contained a movement away from the repetitive, non-symbolic emptiness towards an as yet rather vague re-establishment of symbolic linking between the traumatized parts of the inner world and unconscious, developmental fantasy about primary objects.

Re-establishment of an altruistic object relation

During the following sessions, the verbal dialogue became somewhat less poor, and specifically the nightmares, which Mohammad continued to recount, became still more detailed. I understood this development thus: his pouring out of long-held bitterness and desperation by now had created sufficient containment in the transference to enable him to get in touch with the primary resources of his unconscious world.

The following dream, which occurred some time later, made space, if only for a moment, for the relation to a loving, protective, but in the wake of trauma destroyed, fatherly authority:

> Mohammad is fleeing with his family through the usual mountain[s]. Many soldiers close in upon them. They reach a steep mountain[s], built entirely of wood. They try to climb the mountain,

but the lower part is too steep. His father helps all of them up. They all reach safety on the mountain, except his father, who is shot dead by the soldiers. Mohammad wakes up in anxiety. He has no spontaneous associations to the dream.

This is still a horrifying nightmare, which in most details is like the original post-traumatic nightmare. However, it held more hope than the initial dreams. In this dream, a few details are symbolically elaborated and pave the way for a hope of reparation. In his imagination, Mohammad had created a mountain built not of stone, but of a less massive and constant material—trees.[5] The specific meaning of this detail was never disclosed, but this is probably less important than the fact that Mohammad's ability to create unconscious symbols seemed to be waking. In the dream, a good paternal object is restored in the inner world and the self consequently is able to survive, if only for a moment. The solution of the dream allows for an unconscious expression of anger and revenge relating to the father. This may be understood from a developmental perspective or as some revenge for past and present problems, but either way, it seems likely that guilt and shame in relation to the emotional dilemma of the hostage episode also played a part. It is possible that the dream also shows signs of an initial understanding of the fact that the political activity of the father might have altruistic connotations, a dimension which in the long run might hold the beginning of a change in his relation to the father.

Personal historical identity and the conspiracy of silence

The dream recorded above seems to mark the beginning of a new phase in the therapeutic process. In the following period, the focus thus shifted to Mohammad's attempt to establish a personal understanding of his own and his family's past. He continued to recount still more varied dreams. He still avoided talking directly about the past, but he began spontaneously to relate a few of these dreams directly to memories of specific chains of external events. This development made it clear that Mohammad, unconsciously, felt bound by a family alliance not to name

---

[5] In my later reading of this, it occurred to me that the vital capacity of a mountain built of trees is the presence of what once was a living organism.

by words the most traumatizing memories. Later in the process, we were able together to understand this in the light of an unconscious anxiety that if the self acknowledged the thought that the father was partly to blame for the traumatic burden on the family, then this thought in itself would destroy the good parts of the already strained relationship between the parents. This unconscious dilemma seemed to have contributed to the difficulties in overcoming loss and trauma.

The tendency described earlier on, towards an unconscious conspiracy to avoid consciousness and remembrance of trauma, will affect the relationships between parents and children (Adelman, 1995; Krystal, 1971; Almqvist et al., 1997). For children who grow up under a dictatorship, this unconscious tendency may be enhanced by the parents' conscious limitation of the information given to the children, in a realistic attempt to protect the family and the child from real, external persecutors. However, long after the external necessity has ceased, this policy of silence may live on for psychodynamic reasons, and thus prevent a possible clarification of the post-traumatic confusion of the child as well as contribute to maintaining a persecuted state dominated by splitting and denial.[6]

In the later part of the therapeutic process, Mohammad often returned to a specific childhood memory, which he recounted with a smile as a "cosy" story of the kind which may form part of the family's mythology about the development of the children, and which is lovingly retold on special occasions:

> Mohammad relates that when he was about four or five years old, he and his classmates were to celebrate the country's dictator by calling him, in chorus, "our great father". He did not understand why they were supposed to say this and went home and asked his mother if it were true that this man was his father. His mother replied, "No, your father is your father," which Mohammad went back to school and said. The teacher told him off, and his mother was summoned to a difficult meeting concerning Mohammad. He ends the story by saying that from that day on his parents were very careful not to say anything to him concerning similar subjects.

---

[6] An autobiographic description of this tendency may be found in Rachlin et al. (1990).

This, and similar stories recounted by other children and parents from countries where the form of government is one of absolute dictatorship, in all their simplicity seem to highlight the mental confusion that may be created for a child when its inner tendency to omnipotent, magical thinking is supported and strengthened by an outer, societal practice shaped by similar omnipotent tendencies.[7]

Later, it transpired that Mohammad's recollection of this event was associated with unconscious guilt and shame, in view of the fact that he, with the omnipotent egocentrism of a five year old, saw himself as the reason for the constant persecution of the family. With his more rational 15-year-old self, he knew very well that the causes of the persecution were different and that they were tied up with the family's history over generations, but it did not change his unconscious view. His feelings of guilt were further strengthened by the hostage episode, in which his father in the outer reality, and repeated in the dream recorded above, risked his life and faced prison and torture to save his son.

Mohammad's tendency to avoid memories of trauma and loss seems to involve introjection and identification with silent parent figures, as well as an inner emptiness stemming from the fragmentation of the ability to create inner symbols and thus the ability to mourn the loss of primary objects. Working through this turned out to be essential for an understanding of his continuing depression. This work was initiated by the following dream:

> Mohammad starts the session by talking about the educational and occupational possibilities from which he, as a refugee in Denmark, feels cut off. He thinks that the teachers and other people in authority do not believe in his abilities, since he is not allowed to go to high school because of his difficulty in learning Danish. He says that he has lost three years of schooling because of war and flight, and then recounts the following dream:
>
> He dreamt that he was back at the asylum centre where they used to live with a number of other refugees in a big old house, which in some ways seemed to resemble a castle. In the dream, the centre was quite ramshackle, empty, and without glass in the windows. He entered the house and wanted to go into the family's

---

[7] A similar description may be found in Garbarino and Kostelny (1996, p. 39).

room, but a strong wind came out of the room, pushing him back, so that he could not get in. Having recounted the dream, there is a short pause after which he says that he had seen on the television the previous day that his country is preparing for war.

Together, we succeeded in understanding the inaccessible room with the door that could not be opened as an image of the real, external obstacles to integration, with which a rather hostile and inhospitable society met him and other young refugees.

At a more fundamental level, the vision of Mohammad's dream can also be understood as a metaphor of the inaccessible mental space in which it is possible to think and relate meaning to experiences of war, overwhelming trauma, and grief. Thus, at this point in the process, it was becoming increasingly clear to me, and at an unconscious level seemingly also to Mohammad himself, that he paid dearly for his denial of traumatic memories with a severely decreased vitality and ability to learn. In the moment of the transference, the dream could moreover be seen as a plea to the therapist to leave this door firmly closed, as he was anxious that opening it would release war and destruction in both his inner and his external world.

The fact that Mohammad was now able to dream and to recount his dreams within the framework of the therapeutic relationship may be seen as an expression of a growing wish to repair the inner dialogue between the self and its objects. This was made clear by a later dream, which turned out to initiate a new phase in the therapeutic process:

Mohammad starts by saying that he believes that the reason for his difficulties in learning Danish is that it makes him feel funny inside, as if he all of a sudden is not himself. It is difficult to explain how, but it is as if he is suddenly able only to listen to what others say, and is unable to say anything himself. He wants to take part in what is going on, but he cannot. He seems to be somehow paralyzed. He then recounts the following dream:

In the dream, his beloved grandfather returned. The grandfather had been executed by the regime before the escape of the family. In the dream, the grandfather was standing in a group with other lost members of the family. Removed a little from them stood Mohammad himself with his parents and his sister. For a long while, the grandfather and the others just stood there, their faces turned away. Nobody spoke. They were all dressed in black. Finally, the grandfather approached Mohammad and his family and said aloud, "But why didn't anyone say anything?" after which Mohammad woke up in a mood which he describes as "all black".

From his following associations it becomes clear that the grandfather, in the father's absence, was the anchor to which the mother and children had clung. When the grandfather died, Mohammad did not understand what had happened. He says that no one told him about the execution because it was too dangerous; he was just a child, ten years old, and might accidentally say something in school. He then thought that the grandfather might have died from a heart condition. He remembers that his parents kept crying, his father became ill, and his grandmother died shortly afterwards. But he was not sad because he could not understand anything; he almost did not care. He then mentions that the grandfather had a bird that could speak, but it also died a few days after the grandfather. Mohammad saw the dead bird at the bottom of the cage, and it was as if something within him went dead. This was the same thing that happened when he had been taken hostage the year before. Thoughtfully, he says that it reminds him of the way he now feels in class when he is unable to take part in the conversation of the others.

The traumatic "glass case" from within which Mohammad seemed to be able to sense his surroundings, hearing and seeing them, but not being able to cross the barrier and take part in them, seemed to have become a fixed pattern of reaction, which helped isolate the overwhelmed part of the self but also kept him isolated from his social surroundings. In the dream, he is unconsciously able to establish a meaningful connection between this pattern of reaction and the silence of the adults, which in the past had deprived him of the emotional support needed to mourn his grandfather.

The hostage trauma and the dream work

A meaningful, symbolic processing of the critical hostage trauma did not occur in the manifest content of Mohammad's dreams until late in the psychotherapeutic process. A precondition for this was probably that the initial work with Mohammad's dreams of persecution had made possible a gradual reparation of the unconscious linking with good objects, as in the dream of the altruistic paternal figure who sacrifices himself to save his family, and in a larger sense, his people. This development again seems to have made possible a movement from the paranoid-schizoid realm of the trauma to the capacity of the depressive position to mourn losses, as shown in the dream recorded above.

My presumption that at this stage, a significant inner change was taking place vis-à-vis the objects, was supported by external information from the parents and teachers. At home, his parents reported that Mohammad had become a happier and more open, but also more actively protesting, young man. At school, his teachers felt that Mohammad's motivation to learn and his concentration were significantly improved. He still had problems learning Danish, but less than before, and he had improved in his other subjects as well.

This development seemed to culminate in the following dream, in which Mohammad for the first time seemed able symbolically to link the unsettling residues of the hostage episode with an unconscious, Oedipal imagination.

The current external context of the dream was an upcoming school outing abroad. Mohammad's parents had given him permission to go and the necessary money had been granted. However, due to his status as a refugee, some problems had arisen concerning his passport and visa. Although these problems were about to be solved, Mohammad was very anxious and doubted that everything would fall into place. Clearly the trip and the related problems had triggered the earlier, traumatic anxiety concerning flight, capture, and survival, leaving Mohammad feeling once more thoroughly unprotected against evil forces:

> Mohammad starts the session by relating that at a teacher-parent meeting at school, his teachers had said that his work was much improved, and maybe after all he would be able to enter grammar school as his marks had improved in most of his subjects, although not as much in Danish as he had hoped for. Then he says that last night he had a really bad nightmare, maybe the worst he had ever had. Waking up, he felt as if a hand were squeezing his heart.[8]

---

[8]The specific wording used by Mohammad probably reflects his very direct translation into Danish of the elaborate imagery of his mother tongue concerning overwhelming anxiety and despair.

In the dream he and his family were together aboard a big ship. Then a thief came and took his little sister hostage in order to force them against their will to do something. The thief held the sister over the rail and threatened to let go of her. Another ship arrived and, as the two ships collided, the little sister was squeezed into two halves. Mohammad and his mother cried and cried. They took the little sister to a huge room and laid her on a bed. In the room there were other people who had also been split in two halves. Some of them were Danish. His little sister began to talk, even though she was still in two halves. His mother placed the two halves in an aquarium full of water, saying that the water would make her whole again. The sister looked like a little fish through the glass of the aquarium, but she would never be able to leave it or the huge room again, because then she would go to pieces once more. A loud and droning voice coming from somewhere said that it would happen again. Mohammad shouted angry words against God, after which he woke up, trembling with anxiety.

He comments spontaneously that maybe something evil is going to happen to his sister; maybe this dream is a bad omen, also because the worst possible thing one can do is to accuse God.

The complex psychic work of this dream is far removed from the simple repetitions of persecution and escape in the early dreams. Even without entering into specific details, the manifest dream-content points to an improved unconscious ability to link the traumatic feelings relating to the hostage episode to ordinary, symbolic dream-thought relating to object relations concerning, for instance, sibling rivalry and bad, colluding parental part-objects. In the following analysis, I will focus primarily on the trauma-related aspects.

In this dream, Mohammad in a displaced form allows himself to relive aspects of the hostage episode, casting not the self but the little sister in the role of the victim. The dream-work of this 15-year-old boy seems to revolve, at one and the same time, around age-related developmental aspects and trauma-related aspects. From a developmental perspective, the dream can be understood as revolving around the possible dangers of separation-individuation, in this case leaving his family to travel abroad. From a trauma-related perspective, the dream may be seen as an investigation of the possibilities for reparation of the traumatized self, healing the split of the little sister. Thus the self is unconsciously thought of as gone to pieces, in the dream depicting the splitting and alienation of the self as a physical, sensory bound experience. Furthermore, the traumatized self is left in isolation behind an insurmountable contact barrier, in the dream signified by the two halves of the sister behind the glass case of the aquarium. According to the statement of the dream, the traumatized self must stay behind the protective glass, not able to enter the surrounding world, because otherwise it will again become fragmented, that is, it will be flooded by trauma.

At this point in the process, it was possible for Mohammad to explore his ambivalent feelings towards the therapist as these were contained in the image of the large room in which dissociated people are repaired, and in which Danish people are also present. On the one hand, Mohammad longs for a shared identity with the therapist and Danish society, but on the other hand he feels torn between the old traditional and the new Danish parts of his identity. This inner conflict is probably reinforced by a fusion between an age-related thrust for separation-individuation and a trauma-related, claustrophobic tendency to deny his dependence on the therapy and the therapist. In the dream, he seems to ask if the traumatic split may be healed again, or if the self is forever doomed to be confined in the special "aquarium" of the therapeutic space. In this context, maybe the angry, accusing yelling at an absent father/God near the end of the dream is probably to be understood as an expression of a necessary, but also terrifying mobilization of anger, related both to the traumatic assaults and to a healthy, age-related need for rebellion and for making up one's own mind on authorities within and without the family. At this stage, Mohammad was getting into contact with his own need for a personal revision of family myths, norms, and values.

In the dream described above, it is noteworthy that apart from the initial mention of "his family", the father is not directly present, just as he was often physically absent during Mohammad's childhood, for instance when the boy was taken hostage. It is my experience as a therapist that a number of young boys and adolescents from traumatized refugee families show a tendency to unconsciously avoid full masculine identification. This tendency seems to be linked with denied thoughts about the grown-up self's possible involvement in political activities with a related risk of further trauma. The upbringing of these children and adolescents is characterized by a combination of an often absent but also very domineering father. Moreover, many children have themselves been assaulted or witnessed assaults that were primarily carried out by men. The subjective traces of this external reality seemed for Mohammad to have had extensive, damaging consequences for the ability of symbolically fantasizing about object relations, which apparently went hand-in-hand with difficulties in solving developmental conflicts at all levels.[9]

Mohammad dreamed his dream in a wider developmental context characterized by a combination of external demands for individuation and still new, painful memories of the subjective traumas of the past. These emotional dilemmas were thus also related to an anxious and guilt-ridden opposition and resistance towards the identification of the self with the philosophical realm of the family.

As I hope to have made clear, over the course of time it became possible to discuss the unconscious meanings of the nightmares with Mohammad. The insight he gained from these discussions seemed to be of valuable assistance in his partial integration of the traumatic split. Over the course of the therapy, Mohammad's depression and nightmares seemed to dissolve and disappear, regardless of the fact that throughout the process he refused to talk more directly about especially traumatizing experiences. It is likely that Mohammad would have profited from a longer and more intensive treatment, but since his motivation was weak and solely based on the wish to get rid of disabling symptoms, he would neither be convinced to meet more frequently, nor to continue the treatment once his symptoms abated.

Concluding remarks

The effect on the personality of developmental adaptation to the chronic anticipation of danger and abuse as conditions of life may, in psychotherapy, be reflected in passive-aggressive modes of relating especially in a numbed and dead atmosphere in which time and thinking are annihilated together with any possibility for development. In this deadlock the therapist may urgently feel the external, traumatizing events of the past to be present in the here-and-now of the session which are not yet possible to address. This urgency may be what prompted Gaensbauer (1995)

---

[9]That is as related both to separateness–interdependency, individuation, and Oedipal dilemmas.

and Sutton (1991), quite early in the process, to confront the child with denied information concerning the external events of the past. In the case presented above, I took the opposite stand and did not act upon the urgency felt in the counter-transference, but rather understood this as an urgency concerning how to make possible a bearable dialogue concerning the unspeakable and unbearable.

My experience-based conclusion, therefore, is that in therapeutic work with massively traumatized children and young people, there often seems to be a coincidence in time between reported changes in the behaviour of the children in their external reality as described by parents, teachers, etc., and the point in the therapeutic process when the child or young person becomes able unconsciously to forge a link between imagery related to delayed psychological processing of traumatic experience and material related to ordinary, developmental, object-related fantasy. The interpretation of this may well be that, as symbolic dimensions are added to the fixed traumatic traces, reparation of the broken link between the traumatized and the non-traumatized aspects of the personality become possible. The therapist's containment and symbolic understanding of the reparative dimensions of post-traumatic nightmares as well as of repetitions in play may thus be seen as a "royal road" to reducing the trauma-related, dissociative split in the personality.

In the recorded therapeutic process, talking with the young person about a repetitive, post-traumatic dream after a relatively short while seems to set off a remarkable development in the therapeutic process. Like Lansky et al. (1995) and van der Veer (1993), it is my experience that the post-traumatic nightmare holds in its imagery a possibility for the development of useful, verbal metaphors concerning overwhelming trauma. This may be carried out without verbally going into details concerning cruel, external events. In the course of time, such dialogues not only seem to create a change from the repetitive, rudimentary symbolism of the post-traumatic nightmare to the creative variation of the ordinary dream, they also, not surprisingly, seem to contribute to a liberation of the young person's progressive vitality and drive.

My experience as a psychotherapist with this group of young people is thus that the apparently factual images of the post-traumatic nightmare often hold in the peripheral details the beginning of a symbolic language in so far that in these fragmented details, there may be hidden a link to the young person's fragmented attempt to recreate a symbolic meaning. If the therapist can successfully motivate the young person to focus on their nightmares, the dream thoughts and the therapeutic process seem to progress hand-in-hand. The content of the post-traumatic dream might never be just a repetition of trau- matizing sense impressions, since subjective meaning may have been added to one or more, seemingly unimportant details. In the course of the therapy, these details may change; new details may be added while others are left out, or they may change size or place. These, often very subtle variations in the manifest dream content may be understood along the line of the principles used to understand post-traumatic rep- etition in play.

It is essential then that the therapist be aware that the post-traumatic nightmare, regardless of its stereotypic form, deals with a continu- ity of emotionally painful themes as a whole: the single dream con- taining references to past, present, and future, just as is the case of the ordinary dream. Below the surface, the condensed repetition of a traumatic theme from the past may thus link the assaults of the past to present problems which have certain emotional likenesses. In this sense, the most marked difference between the post-traumatic and the more ordinary nightmare lies in the fact that aspects of certain exter- nal, critical events are given prominence in the visual language of the post-traumatic nightmare.

The post-traumatic nightmare may be seen as an unconscious attempt of the child or the young person jointly to work through certain catego- ries of traumatic and/or painful themes, since these emotionally may replace each other in the dense, unconscious realm of the subjective life history. Thus, Lansky and Bley (1995) for example discovered that the day residues of the post-traumatic nightmare might reflect unconscious shame and narcissistic humiliation relating to the present, everyday life of the dreamer. They conclude that the post-traumatic nightmare con- tains a dream-work the function of which is to re-establish the self as intact and dignified, given that the dreamer unconsciously prefers to transform shame and humiliation into the lesser evils of anxiety and terror. They further suggest that although the post-traumatic nightmare contains intense survival anxiety, the fundamental, narcissistic balance of the dreamer is not seriously threatened.

In the case material presented above, and in correspondence over my therapeutic experience with this group of children and young peo- ple in general, a more object-related tendency seems to apply, meaning that the nightmare presents both the self and the primary objects as interacting in relation to an external, overwhelming danger to life which poses a threat not only to the survival of the self, but also to that of the objects. In the unconscious dream-work of the child or young person can thus primarily be seen attempts to engage the primary objects and, in the transference, the therapist as actively taking part in the reparation of fragmented object relations. Unconsciously, the young person thus seems to try to re-establish the parental objects as dignified, affectionate figures that are in some sort of control of the traumatic events. This picture may be in sharp contrast to the child's earlier experiences of torture-related assaults on the family, to the child's present experience of his own everyday life, such as the parent's personal state and ability to take care of the child after having endured torture, and finally to the humiliations which the child and the family might be subject to, considering the xenophobic and racist tendencies which can currently be witnessed in Danish society. This difference between Lansky and Bley's (1995) findings concerning adult war veterans, and my own concerning traumatized young refugees, should probably primarily be understood against the background of children's real and emotional dependency on primary parent figures, including the fact that parents and children have usually experienced the traumatic events together. However, differences in psychoanalytical orientation and therapeutic procedures may also have played a part.

CHAPTER SIX

The rupture of links in the context of migration: open-mouthed and sewn-mouths[1]

François Fleury and Shadman Mahmoud-Shwana

> *When the counter-investment of the sensory organs is lacking, then the traumatic impression penetrates without resistance into the psychic organism and remains there, resistant, like a long-lasting post-hypnotic suggestion.*

> —Sandor Ferenczi, February 24, 1932

Introduction

How we talk about ourselves: narration

The rationale behind this first section is that in psychotherapy, the cure derives from an exchange of words, the words people use to talk about themselves. Taking this as our hypothesis, we looked at the "faculty" of

---

[1] This text is the fruit of 22 years of psychotherapeutic practice, working in Switzerland with migrant populations from areas suffering conflict or political unrest. It has been written in collaboration with a friend who has worked as an Iraqi Kurdish interpreter and political scientist and with whom I work for the "Appartenances" association in Lausanne.

narration in relation to the "faction" of the heroic cycle. Campbell (1978) and Ricoeur (1988) both described this relationship when they sought a narrative prototype which used the heroic cycle as background and narrative framework for recounting personal history.

In our daily lives, we all tell each other our stories, the role of the listener being no less important than that of the speaker. As two people interact, the speaker seeks to obtain the listener's attention by using all the strings to their bow of knowledge about them. The speaker asks him or herself a series of questions about the person, their words inviting comment on, for example, what their objective is, what their lifestyle is like, and what the listener's social rank is. In parallel with this, the speaker uses their emotions expressed through hierarchically constructed language. The speaker is literally creating a bridge between actual lived experience and the mythical images belonging to their particular culture in order to define their *status as a person*. This status is established mutually therefore, during oral interaction. These ideas are clearly expressed by Ricoeur (ibid., p. 298) when he states that: "Reformation by narration reveals an aspect of knowledge of self that largely surpasses the story; keeping in mind that the self does not know itself directly but solely indirectly and that it is detouring through all kinds of cultural signs that shows us the action is symbolically mediated."

Thinking of the status of a person, it is interesting to develop further the notion of "person" as seen through the eyes of the French language. In French, as in some other languages, the notion of *personne* has particular resonance because it can indicate both the status of "being somebody" but also the "complete absence" of a person. This resonance surrounding the notion of the person "being present and/or absent" gives the story of Ulysses and the Cyclops[2] a new significance, focusing attention on the particular play on words used by the adventurous hero to trick the Cyclops and escape the extreme violence that many of his sailors had been subjected to in being torn apart by the monster's voracity. In his text entitled "Le Calvair, IX, 170", Alizard makes some interesting comments about the translation of the name Ulysses, highlighting the ambivalence of the play on

---

[2] Collège de France: Jean-Pierre Vernant, *Ulysse en Persone*, DVD réalisation Gilles l'Hôte, 52 mn, VF, Dorian Films.

words and names.[3] In brief, his analysis suggests that we talk about ourselves and our status as a person by referring indirectly to the *heroic functions* that exist in our cultures.

The function of the heroic cycle: victorious and/or vanquished

What becomes of the story of the victorious?

The heroic cycle describes an individual who emerges as champion from a series of adventures. The adventures of Ulysses have been used as a prime example, focusing also on the ambiguity surrounding the name. To emerge victorious, Ulysses uses trickery and subterfuge combined with a warrior's strength, the "Ira". "Ira" is a mythical representation of strength used as a means of becoming what human history seeks, a winner. This concept will be developed further in the next section.

Looking more closely at the idea of the heroic function of "winner", it seems that the ultimate ruse is to transform an uninspired story of the potential victim or the experience of fear into a story of strength and victory. Once the focus of this kind of story has become clear, it also becomes worthy of being discovered and talked about. The heroic principle is the

---

[3] http://mul.club.fr/mul23-2.htm *Le Calvair, IX, 170 Une note sur la traduction*. According to Alizard, Ulysses could be considered as "the Harassed" and "the hunted" or even as a "martyr" evoking pain, torment and affliction, the book of Homer carrying the title of *The Chase or the Hunt*. In parallel, phonetically the words *odos, odeusimos, odisma, oditès* are close to the word "voyage" or "going far" and, by extension, could refer to the name Œdipe. This interlinks with the idea of "walking" (Oedipus meaning "swollen feet" or "lame"). At the same time, the word "knowledge" (*oidas* from *eidô*) means "seeing" or "piercing the vision". It is not surprising, therefore, if the Greeks called enigmas "thoughts that go sideways" or "crablike" (since who else could "pierce" an enigma, such as that of the Sphinx, other than a crab or Œdipe?). On the other hand, the name of Ulysses carries many contradictory meanings, ranging from "voyage", as mentioned above, to "finding the right road" or "deportation". The contradictory senses of "being led away from the right road" and the literal sense of the odyssey as "a road of the cross" suggest the sense of "Calvary"; Ulysses's creditors forced him to endure a calvary, the Odyssey, *odussamenos* on the road of the cross, Odos. Returning to the French "*personne*", Vernant and Frontisi-Ducroux recall in *Ulysses in Personne* that the name Outis is a hypocoristic name given to him by his parents and close companions and is also literally his "little" name; the "minus" or "little thing" or, as Polyphemus would say, "worthless." Ulysses actually says in his speech to Polyphemus, "My comrades and my family say that I am less than nothing." This does not correspond to the meaning proposed by Alizard (2001, web) when he translates this sentence as, "My comrades and my family have called me nobody—'*personne*'—that is why I tell you my name is nobody."

passing of trials (Houseman, 1986), each of which seems more impossible than the last and often requires great shows of strength and bravery. Those qualities of strength and bravery, moreover, are continually justified in the name of the "authority" of "being the author". Defeat is rare.

Bellerophon,[4] which means "killer", who was given his name after he killed his brother, Belleros, is another example of such a winner hero. In an attempt to escape, he goes into exile where he is welcomed, as tradition requires, by the local king who discovers his visitor's secret. Because Bellerophon is his guest, the king cannot punish him but instead decides to give him the formidable task of destroying the highly sophisticated and enigmatic Chimera. To the king's surprise, Bellerophon succeeds in his task and so removes all the constraints and burdens thus far imposed upon him. His full rights and authority are restored and he becomes a hero. As a reward he is also offered the hand of the king's daughter in marriage. Later in life, he continues down his path of heroic challenge and finally this leads him to face the gods. In the end, he is thrown from his horse, Pegasus, and is returned to what is described as the lowliest state of mankind; sickly, sad, and abandoned by all.

Bellerophon had to arm himself with the strength and courage of human endeavour in order to fight and defend himself from becoming a predator and, at the same time, from becoming prey.

Warrior strength

> Thus we see Aries, plague of men, marching to war
> Followed by Phobos, his strong intrepid son,
> Who puts to flight the strongest warrior.

—*Iliad*: XIII, 298–299

As mentioned above, *warrior strength* is a mythical force, a belief and instrument used by heroes so that they can become what human history seeks: a winner.

In Norse mythology, *berserkgang* also refers to enormous strength or fury and is represented by the symbol of the bearskin which confers on the bearer the belief that they are invincible. This invulnerability,

---

[4]Grimal Pierre, *Dictionnaire de la mythologie grecque et romaine*, PUF, Paris. Bellerophon, who managed to cheat death, was a descendent of Sisyphus.

as described by Dumezil (1969), refers to a warrior strength that overwhelms anyone who approaches.[5] It drives them mad, consumes them, carries them away, and inhabits them. A practical example of this from a psychotherapeutic session was given by a survivor of the Balkan wars who, describing the terrors he had experienced, related, "They sent back the bodies of two of our soldiers, heads cut off and deposited on their bellies, their sex cut and put in their mouths." Descriptions of battles are bespattered with images of cruelty, violence, and fright. This taste for blood, found over and over again in these stories, is just a glimpse of the capacity of the human imagination to produce what is morbid and demented. Dreams or nightmares are fostered in the lives of people who have lived through violent and extreme events. Similar stories are continually recounted in children's television films where the roles of good and bad are clear, and miracles are played out in favour of the hero. *Spiderman* and *Batman* are two examples of this.

A similar force is described in the myth of Perseus (Clair, 1989), but this story also invites us to look at how warrior strength can be used to freeze or paralyze. The Gorgon Medusa is a source of terror. She has serpents for hair and mesmerizes anyone who looks at her, turning them to stone (Freud, 1985). When Perseus fights the Gorgon, he uses a mirror shield given to him by Athena (we will return to the story of Athena later) to reflect the image of the Medusa on the centre of the shield. The reflection acts as both weapon and protection (Ferenczi, 1923). The terrible power of the Gorgon's gaze is reflected back to its owner, back onto the enemy therefore, and the Gorgon is turned to stone. Perseus

---

[5]The etymology of the term *berserk* is disputed. It may derive from *bare-sark*, meaning "bare of shirt" and refer to the berserker's habit of going armourless into battle. The *Ynglingasaga* records this tradition, in reference to the warriors of Odhinn: "They went without coats of mail and acted like mad dogs and wolves" (Sturluson, 1225, p. 10).

The *berserker* is closely associated in many respects with the god Odhinn. Adam of Bremen in describing the Allfather says, "*Wodan—id est furor*" or "Wodan—that means fury." The name Odhinn derives from the Old Norse *odur*. This is related to the German *wut* meaning "rage" or "fury" and to the Gothic *wods* meaning "possessed" (Dumezil, 1969, p. 36). Dumezil refers to this phenomenon as the *hamingja* ("spirit" or "soul") or *fylgja* ("spirit form") of the berserker, which may appear in animal form in dreams or in visions, as well as in reality (Dumezil, 1973, p. 142). Another Odhinnic quality possessed by the berserk is a magical immunity to weapons (Hollander, 1962, pp. 44–45). These notes on the beserker are taken from notes by Gunnora Hallakarva on the website: www. angelfire.com/realm/shades/vikings/berserker.htm.

is victorious. The narcissistic effect has a double image that forces the enemy, in its fearful violence, to propagate fear. According to Bruno Trentini (n. d.) "The face of the Medusa is the reflection of the face of Caravaggio. It is almost exactly the same as the example of Narcissus but slightly different because in the case of the Medusa, the reflection dies while in the new version of the myth, Narcissus does not die, only the reflection succumbs."[6]

A reference was made above to the warrior strength of Athena, the goddess of war, whose cry alone brings terror. She was the daughter of Zeus and Metis who possessed the gifts of creativity and cunning. Metis was swallowed by Zeus, who wanted her gifts for himself, when she was pregnant. According to the myth, Athena was then born from her father's forehead. On the basis of this, he then tried to foster the belief that men, namely himself, had the capacity to give birth. The legend of Athena the Warrior recounts that she came into the world with a mighty shout, "*Apa Chakeon*". This fierce war cry was part of a special technique for breathing in battle that the goddess had offered to warriors. The cry could be interpreted as being linked to her mother's suffering (Vernant & Detienne, 1974). By appropriating the "force", she saves a generative ability to the detriment of her father who is faced with the curse of his parents' and grandparents' incestuous history which, constantly repeated by the generative mothers, results in the birth of Zeus himself. When Zeus comes to power, he throws his father Cronus, in chains, into the land of the dead because Cronus was known to be a patricide, having killed the grandfather of Zeus. By expelling him to the land of the dead, Zeus believed he was fighting against the incestuous tendencies of the gods, against inbreeding and particularly against the declared right of the invincibility of the fathers. It definitively silences the right to commit incest in what Lévi-Strauss sees as the beginning of the rudiments of culture through heroic birth (Jung, Kerényi & Del Medico, 1993), and through establishing some control over marriage, and hence, over living beings.

This brief story uncovers the invisible line of the function of the heroic cycle and its ambivalence by focusing on human appropriation of cunning and creativity. We now need to look more closely at the reversibility of heroism.

---

[6]*Miroir, Mon Beau Miroir*. The article analyses the link between the self-portrait of the painter Caravaggio with the Gorgon.

What becomes of the story of the vanquished?

> *The easiest thing to be destroyed within us is the conscience;*
> *the cohesion of psychic formations in one entity;*
> *thus is born psychic disorientation.*

—Sandor Ferenczi IV 1927–1933 (1982)

Though rare, there are examples of individuals who tell stories of treating terror with terror, as in a "double bind" between the aggressors and the aggressed. One such example is found among the nomads of the Sahara desert. To stop warriors in their tracks and prevent uncontrollable outbreaks of violence, the women who are facing this threat make use of a ruse that reduces the warriors' emotional charge. As the aggressors approach, one of the older women lifts her skirts, confronting the aggressors with her naked genitals. Disturbed by the sight of the mouth of the womb, the aggressors lose their warrior energy and can no longer nourish their thirst for blood (Devereux, 1983). This example is very close to the Gorgon myth.

Apart from this exceptional example, people tell of their personal experience of war and violence using two different strategies. The first strategy describes the warriors who, by imitation, with reference to the hero cycle and its warrior strength, attribute to themselves great power. This power is used as protective armour inspired or supported by the stories of others but, although they are sheltered by these stories, they still remain more or less fragile. Even the greatest warriors, such as Bellerophon, may fall from a flying horse to their death.

The second strategy involves people who do not imitate and do not, or no longer attribute to themselves, this incredible power. The term traitor is often used to describe this category. This is the strategy when the story finishes in a state of post-traumatic stress and it may not be because the person has lived through this experience, they may just have been in proximity to, or witness to such violence that it has shattered their inner integrity. They are homeless in terms of their deepest sense of protection. There are two types of people in this category, the first are "open-mouthed" and the second the "sewn-mouths".

Open-mouthed in astonishment

Those who are open-mouthed belong to the second category described above and have lived through and witnessed violence and war but have remained passive, without this implying that they have been completely inactive.

They are astonished by what they have seen, their mouths wide open and their hands grasped together, unable to participate in the war as hero or potential hero, despite all they have heard and seen of the functions of hero cycles. They have endured destructive violence that has had consequences at different levels. They are the victims but there is no official recognition of their status. The consequences they suffer relegate them to the status of mental illness or psychosomatic symptoms. Instead of official recognition, still today they unfortunately receive the opposite.

Examples of this category include Palestinian children who, unlike their friends, did not take part in the uprisings, the "Intifada", by throwing stones. The first spoils of the warrior are appropriation of the vanquished women through defilement, collective rape, slaying of male children, and forced impregnation. The list goes on. Is it so hard for us to talk about oppression and historical failure, violence involving civilian populations who become the victims of ephemeral heroes, assuming the right to interfere, transform, and eliminate? Will we have to hear the voices of more victims and more stories to be able to condemn or even to judge?

Over the last few decades, sound has issued forth from the voiceless mouths who have stored up their words in their silence, while living astonished and powerless, open-mouthed in front of unexpected austerity. The voiceless sounds have uncovered the hidden world beyond the cries and the fear. Every day, wars, riots, and catastrophes create innocent victims who join the ranks of open-mouthed people. Terror, arriving unexpectedly and with an unexpected capacity for violence, is leaving its mark on these people. They could never have imagined that such violence could become part of their imagined universe. They were not prepared to see and hear events like these and were even unaware as they were happening. They were there and things just happened around them. Often taken by surprise, they continued to hope that eventually it would end. The end has not come as they hoped. The shock of an endless war is in their daily lives. Each day a very intimate part of their humanity falls to pieces as it internalizes the shock. Their inner lives become a store of stony images; mouths cannot pronounce stony words. It is not by chance that an antagonistic Kurdish expression like "stony mouths" should exist to describe this ugliness. The open-mouthed people have been subjected to the violence of fear, of its passage and its touch. These events often leave terrible fragments and traces of memories of dear relatives and close friends imbued with the atrocities that cannot remain hidden indefinitely.

These traces often end up becoming visitors under cover of darkness when these repressed individuals see the faces of their loved ones, often completely devastated. Access is too difficult in the pallor of their sadness, powerless in the face of daily routine because the traces of memory act as curtains which separate their lives and their fragmented and stony inner will to live. There are many people who have endured events of this kind and who have become wanderers, searching for a place where they are welcomed and where they can be helped to reconstruct themselves, to piece together the fragments. The longer this goal is delayed, the longer the world of terror will pursue them with repeated and insistent nightmares.

Through the psychotherapy we offer, we become witnesses to all this, and as such, we see that these voiceless victims are often ordinary citizens who, if they had not experienced such tragic events, would never have consulted healers of the soul. Often "well constructed", their identities are broken into a thousand pieces that are scattered like the pieces of a jigsaw. On each piece of the puzzle, the same scenes are repeated just as each cell of their bodies carries the memory of these events.

Conducting individual therapy sessions with widows from Bosnia,[7] with the help of interpreters, we repeatedly hear traumatic stories accompanied by invasive somatic symptoms and often severe depression. I have noted that the greatest step they have been able to take has been to gather together and create an association where they could meet (Fleury & Gafner, 2000).

Many women have joined the association, driven by the need to secure and defend their right to asylum, and through this social network some have benefited from the partial or complete remission of their symptoms. From being victims, they have taken up the defence of their rights and thus regained their human dignity and personal

---

[7] Radila Memiseviv (1998), *Journal Fémina*. "The war in Bosnia has caused the death of 25,000 people and 20,000 children, the rape of 30,000 women, the exodus of 2 million people, the destruction of 2000 mosques and 8000 schools and the installation of 800 training camps. This is tangible proof of genocide."

validation. This has enabled them to start to set aside the burden of nightmares (Fleury & Gillard, 1998). The Srebrenica women's movement has given them a voice.[8]

In the summer of 2004, a decision was made by the Swiss authorities to deport some asylum seekers. This decision meant that these asylum seekers could no longer remain under my country's protection and the consequences were the reappearance of the anxieties and the return of the night visitors. These consequences were present both for some of those directly affected by the decision and for others only indirectly affected. The phantoms of difference, of exclusion and especially of powerlessness, have resurfaced and this has paved the way to the return of nightmares and illness.

As an example illustrating both notions of open-mouthed and sewn-mouth at the same time, we received the image below in the spring of 1988 from Hallabja in Kurdistan, a region of Iraq. A father is trying to protect his child in a fight between life and death, while breathing in air that smells of mustard and apple, gas from the military planes overhead. No lungs can predict the arrival of poisoned air. He falls, "tight-lipped", his face hidden from the invasive horror. He forgets that the child's face is upturned, towards the sky, reflecting the strange clouds hanging in the blue sky of her first spring. Her open-mouthedness is stony as she gazes at the sky, her eyes frozen until the moment of her death and beyond, no longer protected by her dead father.

In cases like this, and in the case of the women's associations mentioned above, there is a question to be asked. Could the survivors use their voice and avoid being used by the media to symbolize victims? If this were to happen, would it bring any change to their hope of

---

[8]Fleury, F. & Gafner, N. (2000). In order to make their voice heard against the injustice of their treatment between 1998 and 2000, the Association of Bosnian Mothers followed a strategy. Over three months, they placed five lots of flowers with lists of names in front of the Swiss Department of Justice and Police (DJP). The lists contained names of the women who were asylum seekers but whose applications had been refused and so they were to be deported from Switzerland. The head of the DJP of the canton of Vaud subsequently responded to the authorities in Bern, the capital, by refusing to obey the order and extending the stay of these women in Switzerland for a further year. At a later stage, an inter-cantonal petition of 13,000 signatures was presented to the president of the Federal Council, Ruth Dreyfus. The associations of the women of Bosnia decided to offer all 300 members of the National Council of States a hand-made gift. Many of them gave a kilo of salt, a food that had become so rare in Srebrenica that a kilo was valued at about 12 euros.

carving their words in the history of humanity? It is up to us to remain vigilant in facing the burden of the night-time visitors when they resurface, seeking expression once more.

The open-mouthed have unwillingly internalized the exterior violence. Because of its effect on the links between the fragments of the inner being, this internalization leaves traces for a long time in the lives of the human beings it touches.

"Bouche-cousue": sewn-mouth

Every morning while looking in the mirror
I walk through my inner graveyards
In a memory that overflows my life!

I am a traitor, a great one!
My tear-drops dive into the sea of silence.
And I die longing for living.

It's only today that I see the injuries of bullets of centuries
On my soul.
An immense soul as the Ocean …
As soon as I feel the injuries!

Recovery! Let it be …
It is the recovery of a population!
Of the bits-and-pieces of a body
It is treating all the population as traitors
It is the time of the collective shame!

—Shadman Mahmoud-Shwana[9]

The sewn-mouths belong to those who again are part of the second category of people described above who have lived through and witnessed the violence of war and decided to become actively involved. Their mouths were shut, their lips were sewn because they were suspected of becoming, or were seen to be potential heroes.

---

[9]Poem read at the 2.21 Theatre in Lausanne in April 2006.

They are the people who have experienced the torture and physical suffering inflicted by torturers in prisons or camps. These specialists in torture have the ability to force people to talk by assaulting them or exerting power over the most intimate aspects of their humanity. It is well known that the core objective of these torturers is to reduce the human body to "nobody", its intimate links fragmented in every minute detail. These victims may not necessarily have been touched physically, but a member of their family or from their political party will probably have been tortured in front of them or in their hearing. They have been exposed to their cries, to their pain, and to their silence, a silence which moves inner questions about whether it means the beloved person is dead or whether it just means a temporary halt to the torture.

Having endured moments like these, they are now lost in sufferings that go beyond their comprehension. They are terrorized by the idea of letting themselves recount their stories, of talking about what has brought them to this place of opposition and difference, often through a desire to see humanity improved, having been destroyed, hunted down, and denatured.

The stories that have reached us from all corners of the globe tell us that the objective is always to bring victims to the brink of death and then to leave them, beyond repair, to face the unspeakable.

This kind of terror involves interminable daily interrogations which give no answer. Vilification and flattening are the only emotional food available to the captive, and remaining mute becomes the last hope of defence. As a consequence, in the silence of fear, the dry lips are sealed day after day. This is a paradox well known to those who seek to extract information and words; the silent cry as death approaches which emerges from the deepest reaches of one's being. The victim is killed and not killed at the same time. The specialists of torture also know that what has taken place is ineradicable, and that the breakdown will for ever be irreparable. This knowledge remains the ultimate justification for their totalitarian desire for control.

The following is an example of someone who is in this category. A man came to my office accompanied by his wife and an interpreter to tell me a recent story from the Middle East. He is the father of a family of four children and lives in Switzerland in a precarious situation due to the authorities not having responded to his request for asylum. During our frequent meetings, we considered the necessity of meeting with the whole family. The torture he had experienced was such that it took him more than nine months to say just a few words. We obtained some information from his wife who accompanied him to each of our meetings. He had been broken by torturers who had killed his best friends and members of his party; his inner life was made up of cries and nightmares. He would awake abruptly every night from his nightmarish travels and desperately seek reassurance from his wife.

My approach was to observe the facts told to me by the people who were close to him and to take on the position of an inner voice that reformulates and recognizes the ineffable, in the manner of Ferenczi's (1988) "mutual analysis". I let my personal feelings be expressed while taking an inflexible ethical stance regarding respect for others in terms of violence. The patient himself told me very little, as if he were inhabiting a cell in his old jail, yet I felt his suffering; it froze my body with an obscure intensity.

Step by step, through my reformulation, facts and people appearing in the nightmares became his night visitors. His dreams and nightmares became a living hell, filled with corpses and bodies torn apart which invited the dreamer to join them. Like the warriors on horseback, the hordes of the night, his visitors were there, waiting for him to undertake the voyage where words no longer carried any meaning.[10]

Tisseron's text (1992) on shame was extremely useful at this point; its desription of the four stages of change became the main framework for my work.

It appeared to me that my patient was living through the confusion described in the first stage. This is situated in the same place as the terror, where everything is suspended in time and where only fear and pain remain; the feeling of disappearing and of being outside time is expressed as the rape of "me". The lack of being as the suffering is prolonged, and the confused and complex sensations experienced, render the person both mute and without witness. Uncertainty throughout this period is experienced as permanent. This ambivalence makes existential verification impossible and denies necessary compassion.

The duration of this stage is linked to the moment of rupture, to the sudden destruction as the context abruptly changes. In my opinion as

---

[10]Lecouteaux, C. (1999) writes about the Mesnie Hellequin, a legend well known in Europe. Popular belief attributes the ruinous violence wreaked to a troupe of fantastic spirits who rode very swift horses followed by a pack of howling dogs. They are condemned, as a punishment for their sins, to stay on their horses until the world comes to an end.

a clinician, for some victims it could quietly or voicelessly persist a very long time. It could also flourish again, facing new ruptures, following an increase in stress. An example of this kind of new rupture would be when a migrant suddenly faces decisions regarding deportation from their host country when they have built up hopes around juridical procedures to obtain papers. The symptoms relating to their loss can then reappear and a clinical picture of post-traumatic stress emerge.

Concerning the notion of trauma, Ferenczi (1985) writes in his clinical journal that it is an autoplastic, or self-modifying, rather than an alloplastic, external modification reaction to external or internal stimulation. This neo-formation of the self is impossible without a prior partial or total destruction, or without dissolution of the previous self. A new "me" cannot be formed directly from the previous "me" but from fragments that are more or less elementary products of this destruction. In agreement with Ferenczi (1982), himself a specialist in trauma and the type of experience patients from the Middle East have lived through, I have the feeling that the world of nightmares and night-time visitors gradually invades the daytime world and that reality becomes a mixture of both.

It is in this context that the conscience can be understood to have been modified but in a different way to the "ravishing consciousness" or the "pleasure derived from reality". It is nothing but an "economy of survival". Through repetition, emotional discharge is simply a frantic attempt of the body to reconstruct itself and this occurs whenever stress is present, forcing the individual to re-establish themselves. The identity is returned, in a final effort and in the shape of a sacrificial victim, to its existential cry.

It is as if the person's world were entirely exploited by Thanatos while Eros, or desire, is forbidden; as if the price of extreme suffering were the anaesthetization of sentiment. Finally, it is as if life had become a descriptive story of dreams derived from a faded but disturbing reality that sends the subject back to a hyperactive pre-consciousness which deforms the truth.

My role at this point with this patient was to try to give plasticity back to the dream space; to counteract the reining in of desire, the holding back and management of feeling. Faced with the difficult therapeutic task of relieving the immensity of the patient's suffering, I looked for other concomitant reasons which might be linked to his distress. The first thing to surface was a terrible feeling of living and/or surviving while so many friends had been assassinated, but also the fear of having betrayed or not betrayed them and their friendship. The confusion experienced during the sessions of torture was not a guarantee of certainty for him, in his silence. It brought up feelings of remorse and sentiments of shame.

In the meantime, I also finally discovered that my patient had lost his father. He had been strongly affected by this death, and some time before he was imprisoned, he took part in a spiritualistic session to try to enter into contact with his dead father. He had used his youngest daughter as a medium.

At this point, as if saving ourselves from an imminent shipwreck, we changed the technique we were working with, moving towards an ethno-psychiatric approach. This allowed us to look at the fateful situation from another perspective. The night visitors became the more or less benign spirits of the dead who were returning him to the destruction of his father's role. This destruction was an indelible experience of loss, as in the fall of Bellerophon: "*From this day and until his death, alone and hated by the gods, Bellerophon wandered here and there, avoiding the paths of men and devouring his soul.*"[11]

A few considerations regarding the role of the translator/interpreter

If we compare open-mouthed with sewn-mouth, they appear to be two opposing ideas: the first describes the mouth wide open while in the second the mouth is firmly shut. This opposition disappears if we take into consideration the inner value that goes beyond both: the value of silence. Both are voiceless. They live a silence inside that stills or fixes the images perceived from outside.

Being voiceless does not mean that the person has nothing to say. Reflecting on the nuances of the word "silence" in the Kurdish language provides an interesting illustration of this. The word for "silence" in Kurdish is *Bé-Dang* and it comes close to the idea of being "voiceless". It is composed of two parts, *Bé* which means "without", as a form of negation, and *Dang* which means "sound" or "voice". It is not the aim of this article to go into the grammatical detail of this language but the grammatical expression for defining non-living things is *Bé-Dang*. The nuance invites us to access somewhere which goes beyond "silence".

---

[11] Hamilton, E. (1978), *La Mythologie*, Marabout.

The hidden meaning of the word "voice" could, therefore, be seen as the presence of the voices hidden in the silence.

By extension, we might also be tempted to think that sometimes the complete absence of the patient from a session with a therapist could represent the presence of many different signs. For example, the absence of an Iraqi mother who was supposed to bring her daughter for a therapy session, led me to wonder what the reasons underlying this absence might be. This led me to propose the therapists visit her house. We later discovered that they had left Switzerland, leaving their house, which they themselves had wrecked, behind. From the way the furniture was smashed and the dirt and broken toys that littered the floor, it was clear that these were all things the family had experienced before. They had actually talked in earlier sessions about how, in the eighties, wherever they moved, their homes had been destroyed by the Iraqi authorities. All the children were born during this decade.

Moving to focus on questions of confidence, during their sessions with their therapists these people are expected to talk about themselves and this means bringing many difficult issues to the surface. First of all, the term confidence is built around the idea of at least two people being linked by shared, similar feelings. But, as suggested above, links were not lost only with the outside world but also in the inner worlds of those who were open-mouthed or with sewn-mouths. The reconstruction of confidence was likely, therefore, to take some time since migrants take their losses with them wherever they travel. Other losses resulting from the travel itself are added to the difficulties relating to the construction of confidence. It takes therapist and interpreter, who are the first people met by the patient, a long time to re-frame, tighten, or reconstruct the loosened links. All that can circulate in these triangular meetings are performative actions.

On the other hand, still in relation to the notion of confidence, there is the feeling that the migrant will not be understood both because of language difficulties and purely in meaning. This difficulty complicates the work because the intervention of an interpreter constitutes the participation of a third person in the sessions. The presence of the interpreter may well be highly useful from the language point of view but it could also lead to the migrant not being willing to speak because this means extending trust to the interpreter. The vocabulary, pronunciation, and gestures of the interpreter could potentially hinder communication with the migrant. The interpreter may come from a different region to the patient or may speak a dialect which is typical of the area where the patient's political enemies originated. Confidence, therefore, can take a long time to be reinstated.

Another difficulty facing the interpreter is that he or she also needs to take into account the patient's perception of the time of "voicelessness". However short or long the period of shock may be in terms of the normal calendar, to them it feels like an eternity because it has frozen their perception of time, and consequently, their very identity. It is as though the future were perceived as being enclosed. Their identity was frozen at some point in time and they see this as being irreversible. Sometimes, the culture itself participates in fixing, simplifying, and dictating how individuals should deal with the difficulties they face. This means that the patient has the additional problem of listening to someone, the interpreter, who is perceived as no longer respecting the way of life imposed by the culture of origin.

It is important that this further hurdle of the interpreter seen as traitor be taken seriously. An example of how the paths of the cultures of origin can deviate is afforded by the idea that "men never cry". Starting from this baseline, I developed the idea that the river of their words was not only frozen but also burnt and that this was normalized by their culture. This would suggest that they could neither risk letting their words express what they have seen nor their tear-drops express the dangers they were exposed to. The function of the heroic cycle for these victims is played out in its inverse role whereby they do violence to themselves by not allowing themselves to express what would uncover their hidden secrets. One young man in particular, also from the Middle East, gave us a loud and tangible example of this dry-mouth, dry-eyed situation. Before each session, in the presence of the interpreter, he would show us a new part of his body that he had cut to pieces during the night and, talking of suicide, he would proudly give us a cheerfully mocking smile. The task of talking about himself might entail shedding tears from frozen rivers; I could hear the inner voice hidden in the heart of this *Bé-Dang* man, and sense his underestimation of his own suffering, expressed in his brief, deep, and sorrowful breathing in silence. Before translating his silence and transmitting the words emerging from his inner feelings, the inner values beyond his open-mouth and sewn-mouth, I deviated him from the cultural path he had followed up until that moment regarding the concept of men not crying. This was not without risk but I decided to uncover my own wet eyes by removing my glasses and showing my tears without any shame of being a man crying. He was astonished to see another person crying on his behalf. The point here is to invite the patient to question his own culture, whether man or woman.

These tears could easily have seemed to be in serious contradiction with the cherished notion of an interpreter or translator's supposed neutrality. This certainly is something which is highlighted in this third person's professional role, but it is also important that he or she does not in turn become open-mouthed, or with sewn-mouth, voiceless and tearless. Neutrality does not mean the prohibition of words and it cannot prohibit the shedding of tears when someone is exercising their profession, particularly in contexts where one of the objectives of a session is to re-forge the links between human beings. In the example given above, the verbalization of any word would seem potentially to trigger emotion.

While it may seem that I have gone beyond my supposedly neutral role by shedding tears, it was actually a decision to reveal these tears because I thought they would strike at the internal ice nesting secretly in the hidden abysses of the patient. A few tear-drops shed on behalf of a patient unable to cry knocked at the door of his body. Several sessions later, I could feel that those tear-drops had left a crack in the door. This visit to the body by the patient probably allowed him to access his sounds, his feelings, and the harm of his earlier days of withholding words and tears. I could actually feel, while deciding to remove my glasses, that in one way his eyes were full of repentance because of his earlier underestimation of his own suffering and because of mistreating his body by receiving the night visitors. But, in spite of his repeated words of appreciation for my work, I also felt that he was clearly experiencing a contradiction he could not resolve because of my presence in front of him as a member of his culture where men do not cry.

In this role, there are two elements that contradict the definitions of the vanquished hero that could be of interest in terms of the open-mouthed and the sewn-mouth. The first is that the interpreter is the person who talks most in the sessions. It is obvious that because of their function, the interpreter must speak twice as much as anyone else participating in the sessions. The second element is that being bound by the obligations of the profession and unlike the other people present, the interpreter does not refer to themselves as "I" but uses this in reference to the therapist and again to the patient. Because of this repeated use of "I" instead of their own "me", the interpreter becomes a hybrid person in-between the therapist and the patient. In this hybrid space, the interpreter evokes links between the therapist and the patient. This is a very particular space, unknown to the patient, where a person may dare imagine that men can cry. The contradiction derives from a traitor, the interpreter, being seen as a saviour. The role of the interpreter, therefore, offers a new dimension to the vanquished hero, open-mouthed or sewn-mouth, a talkative and wet-eyed person, a traitor who does not use "I" to talk about themselves or their "eyes" to shed their own tears.

This could be seen as a new type of vanquished hero who invites us to revisit the proper meaning of the profession of interpreter/translator; someone who transcends the words in-between the hidden breaths and who seeks the hidden words in-between breaths, looking beyond the black and white and simplified versions of the definitions of a hero. The interpreter/translator is faithful to his profession as traitor, as described by the Latin proverb, the saving of many translators. The interpreter is a traitor if we follow the definitions of victorious or vanquished heroes.

Apart from neutrality, the translator is also supposed to remain faithful to another ontology, even where this could also appear contradictory. This means translating or interpreting faithfully not only the words spoken but also those left unsaid. As well as speaking the patient's language, the interpreter/translator gains access to the hidden voices by distinguishing the mental constructs expressed in the patient's words. The interpreter/translator also speaks the therapist's language which means visiting the spaces between the broken links. This undertaking is transmitted through the mouth, through gestures, and through examples or even through the perfume worn by the interpreter/translator.

In the context of migration, the language spoken by the interpreter and the patient could also be a space where the patient is invited to revisit their country of origin. It is not exceptional to hear that a patient does not speak their mother tongue except during the sessions with the interpreter. It is less exceptional to hear from patients that they do not speak their language of "secrets" with compatriots they meet by chance. Far from their country of origin, the migrants' opportunities for speaking their mother tongue grows less and less. This could be considered to be one of the new contextual constraints of migration with the migrant in danger of losing these inner links. On one hand, therefore, some migrants do not speak their mother tongue through lack of opportunity. For these people, the sessions with the therapist and interpreter, the triangular meetings, offer the chance to speak their mother tongue which contributes to tightening or rebinding the links, especially if a sense of confidence is reinstated between the three people, a confidence that needs to be constructed within the context of migration. On the other hand, other migrants may use their mother tongue when they occasionally meet up with their compatriots and with new friends encountered by chance; this does not guarantee that in this new context any degree of confidence would be reinstated. The patient will not necessarily reveal his or her new personal anxieties related to migration. Patients may not, therefore, speak about their inner anxieties even if they share their mother tongue with others.

The physical presence of the interpreter/translator evokes for the patient a reality in which they thought they had lost all trace. After all the traumas the patient has experienced, this language of "secrets" contributes to the tightening and processing of loosened or lost links. By hearing the translation, the patient rediscovers links with the "spirits of the dead" of his or her ancestors and memories of times prior to the dreadful events. The concepts and words used during these triangular meetings perform the role of actions in that they can reform links. They may be termed "performative" in the sense that the words themselves carry the images which were constructed in the culture of origin. These images are references in the mental structures of the patient. The words act as guides to help the patient revisit the prohibited zones of the memory, a prohibition deriving from when the only mode of survival was through the perception of just two colours, black and white.

During these meetings, the patient encounters a reality that is absent from the paths of the host country, discovering tangible elements of this absent reality. He or she is thus brought back to a reality that is recognizable because of the presence of a therapist and interpreter who are two human beings sharing and witnessing the absent reality.

The interesting thing about these painful visits is that once accepted, they can also be used as guides to revisit the colourful times before the traumas. The process of reconstruction of the inner links can start with remembering that they have ancestors, that they do not come from nowhere. This rediscovery of places and memories allows them to carve out their personal history, just like any other human being.

As the notion of history intervenes, so the sense of life as constructed and situated in people's history takes on growing and intimate importance. I am not talking about sense with a capital "S" but rather about sense in relation to the idea of using words to re-present or bring back to the present the bits and pieces of the senses that have been smashed, dispersed, and condemned to silence by events.

If we think of each word as a speck of invisible dust that carries, some more, some less, a grain of sense, a phrase is thus made up of the accumulation of these little grains of sense that are interlinked in a reconstructed environment which envelops them. In this particular context, the patient relives not only the moments of suffering but also feels the presence of the absent grains that are essential parts of an individual who is living apart from their previous environment. So the places of relived suffering can also become marvellous points of reference.

An interesting example of a space or a country which exists through words is that of a migrant child who has actually never seen his parents' country of origin but knows their language. When I asked the child why he wanted to go to his parents' country, he answered that he had not seen the country for a long time. The difference between "never seen" and "not seen for a long time" seems substantial. The difference is represented by the language the parents taught the child. The child has created an inner space from his parents' words. When the child visited his parents' country for the first time, he met the reality of his inner country. Although he had to visit the graves of the grandparents, the child was finally able to grow up during the short period of the visit, and become what his father termed a child "of his age". This is a country built from words.

The core of this profession is to feel the contradictory senses of words at one and the same time. When an interpreter translates words such as "silence", "absence", or "identity", they are invited not only to think of what is "discovered" by a word but also what is "covered" by that same word and the synthesis of these reflections. They can then determine whether or not the word or silence or a simple gesture can contribute to "recovering" the person who is living in-between "being" and "becoming" at every instant of this triangular meeting.

PART II

THERE WHERE HORROR HAPPENS

CHAPTER SEVEN

The place of compassion in political conflict

Gabriela Mann

Τhis chapter will address problematic issues that arise when working with people who suffer from terror and trauma, and who belong to opposing political camps. More often than not, we are inclined to identify with victims of terror and trauma, since we often consider them to be innocent victims. However, when working with political opponents, it is at times hard or even impossible to identify with them. This kind of work often forces the therapist to face their own preconceived ideas, dogmatic thinking, closed mindedness, and wish not to get to know the patient.

The major issue for discussion in this chapter is what can turn a terminal link, between a therapist and a patient who belong to opposing political camps, into a transformational one. Using concepts developed by Bion (1967) and Kohut (1966), I will address the possibility of transcending differences in the psychotherapeutic encounter, with the goal of ridding oneself of preconceptions and misunderstandings, while learning from the immediate experience. In so doing, it will be helpful to utilize the concepts of emptiness and compassion. I believe this method is applicable in other hostile encounters as well, beyond the realm of psychotherapy.

I will present a clinical vignette to depict a situation that developed between a politically left wing psychotherapist and a patient who is a settler from the West Bank, and therefore extremely right wing. The patient was being treated at NATAL, the Israel Trauma Center for Victims of Terror and War.

The vignette illustrates a transformation from initial dread, contempt, and wish not to know the patient, to a transcendental mode of inter-being. Such a mode of being dissolves the encapsulated mind; it signifies an expansion of the mind and dissolution of immediate boundaries.

Current thinking about terror and trauma

Current thinking about trauma and terror supports the idea that aggression is no longer considered to be only an inter-psychic event. Puget (1989), who wrote about social violence in Argentina, defined three different psychic areas where social violence occurs: the intra-subjective space, the inner space of the individual, the inter-subjective space, a dyad or a group, and the trans-subjective space, that between nations. The aggressive act may exist in any of these spheres or in all of them simultaneously. It is assumed that traumatic situations are linked in a symbolic manner to internalized figures and events from the individual's past.

Yolanda Gampel (1999) coined the phrase "radioactive identification" to serve as a conceptual and metaphoric representation of the penetrations of terrible, violent, and destructive aspects of the external reality, against which the individual is defenceless. The individual internalizes the radioactive remnants of which he is unaware, and identifies with them and their dehumanizing aspects. Later, the individual acts out these malignant identifications which are alien to him, or they are acted out by his children through the process of trans-generational transmission. The power of these destructive forces appears in an unequivocal manner within both the individual and the society.

Other theoreticians who can be briefly mentioned in this context are Eigen and Bollas. Eigen (1999) used the concept "Toxic Nourishment": fusions of trauma and nourishment which mark our lives. Sometimes the balance between them becomes destructive; trauma may be so severe that nourishment becomes less and less possible. In extreme cases, in order to obtain nourishment, the individual is forced to absorb various emotional poisons which are overwhelming to his/her sense of life goodness. Bollas (1999) similarly used the concepts "Return of the Oppressed" and "Inter-jection" to describe what happens to victims of social violence who are exposed to unbearable anguish. When they come to see us, we discover pockets of oppression in these patients, a structure within the self, the outcome of oppression that reveals itself in a particular way and calls for special attention by the analyst. Our mindfulness to these matters may reveal that the internalization of oppression is sometimes deferred and understood as a way of *Nachträglichkeit*. An event later in life may evoke the oppressed, and it will make its entry into consciousness in an unexpected, sudden, and intense way.

What we clearly see in this brief theoretical survey is that when we think about victims of terror and trauma, we need to pay considerable attention to the situation of the recipients of the aggressive act. We have to consider a violent amputation of the continual self experience and the infiltration of the aggressive characteristics into the recipient's psyche. These aggressive trends can take various forms; they can be a repetition of what has been inter-jected into the self or they can transform into aggression against the self.

When we encounter these patients, we are faced with the challenge not to get intoxicated by their "malignant" *Weltanshauung*, not to be seduced into a game of terminal projections and inter-jections, but to try to transform these deficiencies by making it possible to let a new, intersubjective experience emerge. Each side, analyst and patient, may make use of the other's subjectivity, take it in, digest it, and bring it back in a modified fashion. Taking it in is containing it and the modified response is transforming it. But there is more to this. A major factor in this process is the emergence of compassion. Compassion may bring about a transcendental transformation, not on the content level but on levels beyond; something that was unknown is emerging and is allowed to be realized.

The wish not to know

An essential characteristic of coping with traumatic experiences is the wish not to know about them. Where intolerable anxiety, fear, or shame are evoked, such as in situations of trauma and terror, a negative link of knowledge will evolve. In this case, meaning is obstructed, leaving a denuded representation so as to dilute the facts and reduce the pain. The result of such intersection will be, in some cases, the proliferation of lies or distortion of facts, which serve as a barrier to truth. Bion (1970) believed that truth is a permanent source of pain and the human being's capacity to tolerate truth about himself is fragile. The tendency towards evasive action is great, and the mind is always prepared to create distortions of reality to oppose the pain. We can consider that not knowing is not just an individual occurrence. We are all too familiar with group blindness in situations of social violence, blindness to the plight of the victims, and blindness to the pleas of opposing groups. A blind attitude helps to escape social responsibility and avoid pain. It enables the individual to remain "clean" and unaffected. We may consider it as our task, as mental health providers, to support individuals and groups in transforming blindness in analysis and beyond.

One configuration that contributes to the occurrence of not knowing is the phenomenon of "reversal of perspective". This is taken from the well-known experiment of perceptual psychology that consists of the observation of a print that can represent either a vase or two profiles. Bion (1963) uses this experiment as a model of all situations of insight and creativity in which the personality can switch one point of view to another in relation to what is happening. Such capacity to tolerate paradox provides a basis for mental development. In reality, reversal of perspective is a complex phenomenon as the individual tends to remain in one perspective only from which he "sees" the reality. This is not a manifest attitude; on the contrary, it hides behind an apparent agreement and understanding. In practice, we encounter situations where it appears that a patient communicates with the analyst openly, while in fact he does not relate at all to some major traumatic experiences. These experiences are omitted from the dialogue. This kind of discourse cannot lead to genuine transformative contact. Interpretations remain repetitious and empty. We may consider this situation a defensive organization formed to operate against awareness.

Kohut (1971) depicted such a one-sided attitude when he published the radical idea of the vertical split. He posited that narcissistic needs that remain with no sufficient response foster a fragmentation of the psyche, a vertical split. In contrast to the horizontal split, which refers to repression, one finds the coexistence, side by side, of incompatible psychological attitudes ranging from slight incongruence, to a situation which verges on fragmentation. We may see the manifestations of unmodified injury side by side with manifestations of a self that is bound to realistic goals. One attitude is blind to the other. He elaborated further the description of such a state of mind in his extensive discussion of the narcissistically injured person's rage: "The narcissistically injured … cannot rest until he has blotted out an … offender who dared to oppose him, to disagree with him, or to outshine him" (Kohut, 1972, p. 385). For Kohut, narcissistic rage is an indication of suppressed, unmodified narcissistic structures which become intensified as their expression is blocked. Such states often coexist with emotional blindness.

It is interesting to note that Bollas (1992), twenty years after Kohut (1971), described the Fascist state of mind in similar terms: "The core element in the Fascist state of mind is the presence of an ideology that maintains its certainty through the operation of mechanisms aimed at eliminating all opposition" (p. 200). Doubt, uncertainty, and self-interrogation are equivalent to weakness and must be expelled from the mind to maintain ideological certainty. We have to consider that the expulsion of parts of the mind that contradict a certain ideology or maintain doubt must contribute to the mind's flattening if not to its erasing. The mind avoids any vivid encounter because everything is known in advance and there is no space for learning from experience. I have referred to such a link elsewhere as the "Terminal Link" (Mann, 2002).

We have to consider that such cases of fragmentation not only indicate that the contained is unable to use the container productively, but also that the container fails to respond to the emotional needs of the contained/subject. In Kohut's (1991) terms, we could say that the self-object is unable to lend itself creatively to the self's needs. In many cases, this leads to an intensification of frustration in the link between self and other states. A constellation is established that creates an antagonistic attitude, hatred of knowledge, a severe "disorder of the impulse to be curious" (Bion, 1957, p. 107). We can assume that the subject, who experiences an environment that fails to know him, eventually gives up the wish to be known. In these instances, unmentalized elements might be extruded from the mind and evacuated into the body, into the perceptual field, or into the trans-subjective sphere (Puget, 1995), the realm of action and social violence.

While we relate to the patient's difficulties in uncovering the truth during the analytic process, with some understanding and as an expected development, we must also continuously consider the less recognized resistance put up by the analyst to evolution of traumatic knowledge. The analyst has his or her own anxiety, which warns of dangers and the high price which they could pay for coming face to face with the patient's catastrophes. In the interaction between patient and analyst, the patient's projections may induce unbearable feelings in the analyst. The analyst, being unaware of what is happening, feels bewilderment and unease and may be unable to tolerate it. At this point the analyst may violently reject the material, or displace the reaction in some way so as to disguise it. The analyst may evacuate their discomfort by resuming to action in various forms.

We are talking about the vicissitudes in the analyst's and the patient's different states of mind: both patient and analyst have a blinded and an illuminated mind. The blinded mind comes to the forefront in the face of trauma, provoking defensive acting and the preference not to see. In contrast, the illuminated/creative mind is guided by a free flow of empathy, contains the pain, and carries out the analytic work.

Thus, it is vital that we consider both an inter-subjective relationship between two people as well as the intra-subjective interaction between opposing factions within each person's mind. The context is what determines which part is brought out.

NATAL—the Israel Trauma Center for Victims of Terror and War

NATAL was established in 1998 by Dr Yossi Hadar, a psychiatrist, a son of Holocaust survivors and a survivor of the Yom Kippur War in Israel. As a physician, he was exposed to the major suffering of soldiers during this war and was highly concerned about their wellbeing. In NATAL, he wanted to create an independent, institutional setting that could treat Jews and Arabs who were exposed to trauma related to the Israeli-Arab conflict.

The initial thought was that the target population for treatment would be those people who took an active part in wars, such as soldiers or recruited civilians. It was obvious that these people suffered from continuous post-traumatic symptoms: dissociative conditions, mood swings and depression, flash backs, obsessive rumination, sleep disorders, anxieties, and phobias. Often people reported such symptoms without any awareness that their suffering was related to trauma. This notion was validated during the Intifada. It became more and more obvious that not only soldiers showed such symptoms, but also ordinary civilians. In addition, the affected population was no longer just those who directly witnessed the act of terror, but also the "second circle", namely the relatives and friends of the injured, or those who were exposed to acts of terror via indirect witnessing such as through the television or the press. Findings have shown that simply hearing reports about terrorist attacks may lead to traumatic-like anxieties.

The therapeutic conception developed by NATAL is to view the post-traumatic syndrome as a total situation that embraces both the intra-psychic life of the patient and their social functioning. Based on this assumption, NATAL offers treatments on various levels.

A clinical, inter-disciplinary staff offers various kinds of psychotherapy: psychoanalytic psychotherapy, biofeedback, art therapy, movement therapy, touch therapy—very important for people who have suffered burn injuries, and group sessions. Often the treatment consists of a combination of different modes of treatment.

The treatment is offered for an unlimited length of time and does not strive to focus only around the traumatic content. There is an attempt to relate to the crisis as an opportunity for change.

Another possible avenue of access to NATAL is to call a hotline and have weekly telephone sessions on the phone. Such sessions can take place with the same person each time. This is a means of offering treatment to those who are too ashamed to be identified as a "patient" officially, or those who do not wish to openly recognize themselves as "needy". It takes into consideration the link between injury and shame and the emergence of complex feelings of devaluation that come with such injuries: guilt for surviving, for not helping others, for running away, a damaged physical self-image, and so on.

A rehabilitation programme is offered to release post-traumatic victims from social isolation. We often hear from such patients that they feel deserted by their relatives, either because they became a burden or because of the great demands that they have and because of their sense of unlimited entitlement. The NATAL programme offers art classes, yoga, and karate, group activities which vicariously affect the ability to concentrate and be attentive, as well as social skills. An additional option is joining the chat room on the net, where people share their experiences anonymously, ask questions, and find an emphatic echo to their problems.

Finally, NATAL offers services of support, debriefing, and information to people in the community who are directly exposed to catastrophes via their role at work. Here I refer to policemen, ambulance and rescue teams, or hospital employees. To give an indication of the usefulness of such services, I want to mention that there are at present

12,000 telephone calls per year and a case load of about 250 patients in on-going psychotherapy. Three hundred people are using the hotline on a weekly basis.

Clinical vignette

I would like to present a short clinical vignette[1] that can illustrate the process of transforming blindness in the therapeutic encounter with political opponents. The material was presented to me in supervision by a therapist who works for NATAL. The patient was a young woman, doing public service in place of army service in Tel Aviv. She called the hotline of the centre after a terrorist attack in Tel Aviv and complained that she was suffering from excessive anxiety, fear of being attacked, and difficulty in sleeping. She was referred to therapy.

Ester comes from a religious settler's family in the West Bank. Her background is instantly conveyed by her code of dress: long sleeves and long dress with long pants underneath. The therapist noticed her pretty eyes with their sad expression. Ester conveyed immediately that she is doing a period of state sponsored public service against her mother's will, and is not sure whether this was the right decision for her, but she felt she needed to distance herself somewhat from her family. She believes that probably God is putting her on trial for separating herself from her family's wishes, or is punishing her. She also made it clear that she does not know what psychotherapy is about but, given her current discomfort, is willing to try it out.

Consider the following interaction within its social context of severe political stress between the religious, right-wing settlers of the occupied territories and the "lefties" who are opponents of the occupation.

This vignette took place after a year in which Ester had become very committed to the process of therapy. There was a long silence, which was unusual for her. The therapist felt that there was a barrier between her and the patient; that Ester wanted to say something which was hard for her and the therapist mirrored this feeling to her. The patient confirmed her therapist's notion and mentioned that she was very

---

[1] This vignette was also discussed elsewhere as an example of emotional blindness. See Mann (2007), Emotional Blindness and its Transformation. *The Psychoanalytic Review, 94(2)*: 291–313.

angry with her instructor at work, who had criticized her. She described what had happened. She had to give children a lesson about Rabin's assassination and read his autobiography to them. When she came to the Oslo agreement, a partial peace agreement between Israel and the Palestinians, she inserted the following sentence: "In this agreement, Rabin gave the Palestinians weapons to kill my neighbour." The therapist tried to understand whether she was talking about a specific event. Ester explained that it was not a concrete event. It was the intention to kill "all" her neighbours, the Jewish people in the settlement.

The session took place on the actual memorial day for Rabin, a former prime minister, who was assassinated in Tel Aviv by a right-wing activist at the end of a peace demonstration. The therapist felt revolted, flooded by rage and pain and was aware of the growing distance between her and the patient. When she tried to encourage the patient to elaborate more on what she thought, the patient began to present extreme right-wing ideology, which was even more upsetting to the therapist. The therapist reported that she was close to breaking out of the therapeutic setting and involving herself in a harsh political discussion, or immediately interrupting the session, yet she controlled herself and mumbled a few sentences about who is a victim and who is an aggressor. When the session finally was over, the therapist felt confused between the outer reality and psychic reality; she felt immense anger and revulsion for the patient, as well as guilt and disappointment with herself for failing to contain the situation better.

The therapist said she waited eagerly for supervision. It was the first time she had brought this case to supervision. As soon as she started to report on the hour, I expressed my feelings to her: "There is a feeling of catastrophe here; your patient is in great turbulence and you could not find compassion for her; it must have touched a painful string in you."

Following this intervention, the therapist spontaneously unfolded her personal subjective experiences of pain. She recalled her father, who had died two months before. Her father was a Holocaust survivor who wanted to build a better life for himself and the generations to come. As a victim of racism in various concentration camps, every manifestation of violence was unbearable for him. He adored Rabin and his efforts to bring peace. The therapist grew up absorbing these values.

The therapist continued and shared with me that her birthday is actually on the day of the Balfour Declaration, a statement of the British mandate (1917) regarding their intention to establish a home for the Jews in Palestine. She felt that she was the carrier of this declaration and that she is committed to it. There was a pause in our dialogue and she suddenly said: "Ester and I actually share a common element: we were both born in an unsafe place. Both of us are actually exposed to a similar sense of catastrophe. I am concerned about what will happen to the state for which my parents fought bitterly and Ester is threatened about the future of the territories where she grew up all her life." Now we could realize that Ester's pain and her own pain were not so different. It was a moment of encounter with the foundations of each person's deepest fears and mental pain.

Rather than being attuned to Ester's being a victim of circumstances which happened prior to and consequent to her birth, the therapist now realized that she saw her patient as an aggressor who was out to destroy her own fundamental values. She had understood Ester's distortion of Rabin's story at face value, from one single perspective, with no elaboration of its subjective meaning. As the supervision hour proceeded, the therapist recalled how Ester was born after the death of her grandfather and how her depressed mother never held her in her arms. Ester was an unheld baby born on shaky territory. When Ester read the text to the children, she was struggling to maintain both her internal home-base as well as her actual house, which was about to be destroyed. In addition, the therapist's fast intervention concerning the barrier between her and the patient prevented Ester from safely elaborating her suffering and pushed her towards a defensive position. The long lasting cleavage between the patient and her unattended mother was re-enacted in the session, this time vis-à-vis the therapist.

The realization that each of them has her own spiral of personal history enabled the therapist to understand her empathic failure. She realized how her own dread had obstructed her ability to feel compassion for the patient. She understood that external reality and psychic reality were conflated in her mind for a while. The supervision created space to see both the underlying narcissistic injuries of the therapist and those of the patient, and to transcend this knowledge to a broader vision of suffering. The supervision hour ended with an expectation that unfolding the impasse would provide both patient and therapist with an opportunity for further growth. This transformation was not connected at all to the overt content of the hour. It was related to the ability to touch on the underlying spheres of the mind.

Two weeks later, Ester expressed a wish to attend therapy sessions twice a week. She now reported a dream which she defined as a "Holocaust dream": "Faceless people are marching with suitcases in their hands." In her associations, she referred to the future evacuation of her settlement. She was giving a pictorial image to her internal catastrophe, the sense of her home collapsing and the shaky ground. Finally, she said clearly in words: "One day my home will be taken away for ever and what can I retrieve?" Then she added: "The sad thing is that people think about this in terms of ideology. They do not understand the suffering involved." The therapist was astonished; was the patient now dreaming the history of her own father?

In her mind, a faceless patient, labelled as "the settler", became a real person, Ester.

Expansion of mind: a transcendental mode of inter-being

The vignette demonstrates a situation in which a containing function and sufficient empathic echoing transform impersonal phenomena and dogmatic thinking into a truly subjective experience. The supervisor's role as witness and container was transformative in the sense that it allowed the therapist the possibility of holding on, thinking about and "digesting" problematic and painful material. A link of knowledge was established. Let us bear in mind that Bion (1970) portrayed the container/contained link by symbols that imply the existence of a sexually productive pair. In this kind of context, new meaning can be conceived. In the present example, a "now moment" occurred in the sense that the therapist suddenly realized something that was previously blocked out of her mind. If we think once more about the experiment in perceptual psychology, the therapist was suddenly enabled to see an alternative perspective. The transformation that occurred for the therapist enabled a quick renovation of Ester's state of being. She was no longer in a defensive position that drew her into blind ideology; she could let herself emerge and unfold. We may think about Kohut's (1984) notion of the self-object's function in balancing the empathic matrix.

But there is more to it: the vignette illustrates a momentary encounter when blindness is transformed into broad vision, beyond the realm of inter-subjectivity. When the therapist suddenly realized that she and her patient had something in common, that they were both born in an unsafe place, a transformation of a different order occurred. I realized that some radical change had occurred in her mind. Dissolving the most complex boundaries between them as therapist and patient, representing right- and left-wing schools of thought, enabled the therapist to transcend to a different state of mind that is beyond knowledge. The therapist gave up the exclusive commitment to her own subjectivity and her own single-perspective version of history. She was no longer an exclusive self in its self. All at once she was feeling compassion towards all those who were forced out of their places and whose environment is an unsafe one, regardless of their affiliation.

A narcissistic capsule in which the therapist was captive transformed into a broad vision about human fate. Once this freedom of sight was attained, a state of serenity that consists of reconciliation was achieved; the richness of the therapeutic encounter was now allowed to unfold freely. What we are talking about is the transcendental transformation that can occur when compassion is allowed to emerge. To my mind, this is beyond the use of projective modes of communication; it is a different order of relating.

At this point, I want to highlight the radical move of both Bion and Kohut towards transcendental psychology. Bion (1965) coined the phrase "transformation in O" to represent a process of becoming, of intuiting the unknown and moving towards an underlying truth. Becoming O is possible only if a state of "at-one-ness" is allowed to take place. The analyst can achieve the mental frame in which she can be receptive to O, only if she has the capacity to be in "at-one-ness" with it. One might say that this is equivalent to empathy but it seems more complex. It is a form of relating, where open intuition is tuned towards a communion with truth. Kohut (1966) presented a similar notion when he introduced the concept "cosmic narcissism" to describe a state of participation in "supra-individual existence" (p. 266); an expanded sense of self merged within the world. It has to do with a dissolved state of selfhood, a state of inter-being and non-separation from the broader surroundings. It is a situation beyond cohesion and beyond structure. It refers to those unique and cherished moments, when individual narcissism is transformed into an amalgamation of higher experiences of belonging.

In order to reach such states of inter-connectedness, both container and self-object need to empty themselves of their memory, desire, and previous understanding (Bion, 1967), as well as of their own prominent modes of operation and their narcissistic positions. It is not that they need to be literally empty but that they need to be willing to relinquish holding on to their usual tendencies and attitudes. Letting go of their individual and mutual motives allows for a free-floating mind to work in the hour and beyond.

Such an attitude consists of compassion; daring to see painful parts of the reality and not pushing them away, accepting parts of others and of ourselves that are not the ones we necessarily like. What is implied is not being fixated to a dogmatic experience, not being caught up in our own version of reality, maintaining instead an open space and freedom to feel and experience a whole range of emotional states. Bion phrased such an attitude quite radically: "The psychoanalyst should aim at achieving a state of mind so that at every session he feels he has not seen the patient before. If he feels he has, he is treating the wrong patient" (1967, p. 19). This is what Bion means by "without memory and desire".

In Buddhist texts, the concept of compassion is often connected to situations of animosity and not to situations of love. Compassion is not necessarily a function of positive emotions; it is the ability to be in the other person's place, often in his suffering or pain or in his different modus. In our example, this happened twice, first when the therapist said, "I realize that we have so much in common," and following that, when Ester brought her "holocaust dream", a visual image that captured her fate, the therapist's personal history, and the suffering of all the uprooted. She also elaborated later, saying: "The sad thing is that people think about that as ideology. They do not understand the suffering." She recognized now the defensive and blind nature of her own ideology.

In a personal comment, a colleague shared with me some of her thoughts with regard to the draft of this chapter. Among her various thoughtful and personal remarks, she asked: "How did you get there? What were your feelings?" These questions are derived from inter-subjective thinking and deserve to be addressed. Let's look at my intervention once more:

> There is a feeling of catastrophe here; your patient is in great turbulence and you could not find compassion for her. It must have touched a painful string in you.

In this intervention one can identify multiple components, but it is important to notice that the first component signifies a transcendental notion, the recognition of suffering as a broad experience, namely, an experience that includes me, the therapist, the patient, and humanity. Intersubjectivity was not used in its usual sense, but as an idea of supra-individual participation in a universal experience. The other components relate to more common elements, the patient's turmoil (a therapeutic notion), the empathic impasse between patient and therapist (a supervisory notion), and finally, a message of empathy towards the therapist.

What is the nature of this first component which consists of a transcendental mode? Is it a function of intersubjectivity? Is it derived from concepts of the relational field that emphasize interaction and duality, or does it bring out a situation of a different nature? In a Self Psychology meeting, Max Sucharov (2001), in his paper "The Infinite, the Sacred and Contextualism", referred to an "... ultimate cosmic context within which psychoanalytic inquiry takes place". He said: "At the experiential level we are talking about a situation where the infinite or cosmic context that unites us all is felt most profoundly, and where this awareness is fully integrated with our personal subjectivity, allowing us to live fully in the moment with maximum freedom, creativity and vitality." Such a situation consists of non-dual inter-being. Perhaps, as a paraphrase of Kohut's (1966) conception of "supra-individual participation", we can think about a concept of supra-intersubjectivity: intersubjectivity that goes beyond what there is between one subject vis-à-vis another. It stems from intuitive knowledge, when the individual self and his/her subjectivity are relinquished or dissolved into a state of at-one-ment with what is beyond.

So, to come back to my colleague's question, I can only say that when the therapist described the situation during our supervision, I suddenly found myself in a momentary inter-connectedness which allowed for blurred boundaries between the therapist's experience, the patient's experience, and mine as well; as though we all belonged to the same extended humankind. To say "There is a feeling of catastrophe" addresses the sphere which is beyond the particular therapist, beyond the particular patient, and beyond me as a particular supervisor.

What exactly allows for a universal statement at a certain moment is unknown. This kind of awareness cannot be easily explained or justified by a particular process or special concept. Its quality can only be described as a sense of connectedness with a broader sequence of events which is there at a particular moment. It probably comes close to what Bion (1965) referred to as "invariance"; connecting for a fleeting moment with an ultimate reality which is beyond that particular manifestation. One grasps the bigger picture rather than that produced by a particular interaction between two subjects. It might be that this was possible owing to my own personal history, or perhaps the closeness between myself and this therapist, which allowed for such a statement with a universal quality. I can say with more certainty that it is related to my being deeply immersed in the psychoanalytic thinking that considers the transcendental realm and non-dual experiences as essential parts of existence.

I believe that in our example, my comment to the therapist provided her with a "background of safety" that enabled the instant change in her state of mind. She did not need to defend herself, nor did she feel guilt or shame for what seemed a lack of containment on her part. She immediately relinquished her blinded, narrow perspective of the patient. In its place, she retrieved compassion towards herself and could now unfold her own subjective experience and make the unexpected leap to the transcendental mode. The patient responded to the shift in her therapist's mind and changed the sessions to twice a week. Then she presented the "Holocaust dream" with its universal significance with regard to all the uprooted. Ester made her own leap into the transcendental realm.

I hope that this example illuminates the full range of contextuality between the supervisor, the therapist, and the patient. One question remains open though. Can such transcendental transformation extend beyond the rooms of the therapy?

To answer this question, I would like to refer to an additional incident between the therapist and Ester that occurred a year and a half later, during the recent civilian and military withdrawal from Gaza in August 2005. During this period, extremely high tension was felt all over the country. Right-wing people at this point were wearing orange shirts or carrying orange flags to signify that their suffering is reminiscent of the Jews who wore the yellow tag when they were forced out of their homes during the period of the Nazis. Left-wing people were flying blue and white flags, and condemned the right-wing comparison between the disengagement and the Holocaust as utterly absurd.

At one session during this period, Ester entered the room and left her backpack outside. The therapist asked why she did not want to bring it into the room. Ester said that it was too heavy. The therapist offered to help her and they both carried the bag into the room. Ester mentioned that she had come from Meimon, from a violent demonstration of the settlers against the disengagement. The therapist wondered whether she had an orange shirt. Ester responded: "My shirt is in the bag. I left the bag outside. Orange is not needed in this room."

"Orange", a symbol of narrow vision, is now mindfully kept extra-territorially, outside the room. Ester chose to leave the dogmatic mode of being outside the room when meeting with her therapist. Did she totally relinquish the "Orange mode" as an act of transcendence or was she avoiding something when with her therapist inducing a split between various circumstances? We cannot be certain. Yet I believe that the creation of an extra-territorial space for her therapy is a manifestation of trans-contextuality, similar to what Winnicott (1953, 1967) meant by transitional phenomenon, not a function of a split-off animosity. Thus, the therapeutic achievement is that she has realized that she can be different in different contexts and in certain contexts she chooses to eliminate "Orange". She has become mindful enough not to wave the "Orange" flag around in an undifferentiated manner. This is an act of transcendence of itself.

We have to consider the special significance of transcendental thinking. As people who think about how to cure, we ask ourselves what is it that ultimately brings about psychic growth and optimal unfolding of the self. I believe that states of transcendence, when we rise above the concrete and discrete analytic materials, are moments in the analytic setting when we gain authentically new perspectives about our patients. In such moments, containing and empathy evolve into compassion. We are then able to free ourselves from preconceptions, seeing beyond the immediate, while bringing about change that has a fundamentally distinctive quality. This does not happen easily or frequently and therefore needs to be highly valued and ceaselessly cultivated.

Does transcendental experience contribute to the relinquishing of the "Orange mode" in situations beyond the therapeutic situation? Is the therapeutic encounter adding to the emergence of compassion and serenity beyond?

I can offer only one response: that we need to have faith that this is so.

CHAPTER EIGHT

Tell me your story: psychoanalytical trauma psychotherapy in South Africa[1]

Katharina Ley

> In the African *Weltanschauung*, a person is not basically an independent, solitary entity. A person is human precisely in being enveloped in the community of other human beings, in being caught up in the bundle of life. To be is to participate. This is Ubuntu.
>
> —Desmond Tutu

Framework of trauma therapy in South Africa

Today, South Africa is called a society of post-conflict and transition. The new democracy is in its eleventh year after more than 350 years of apartheid. Crime and violence are pervasive and affect every level of society. Since the formal process of political transition and democracy in 1994, there has been a transmutation of political violence into criminal violence. During apartheid, the events of trauma were political ones: assaults, shootings, arrest, torture, murder, disappearances, and

---

[1] Revised version of a paper given at the Conference of the European Federation for Psychoanalytic Psychotherapy (EFPP), Stockholm, July 4–6, 2003, ongoing workshop "Trauma and State Violence".

exile. Today's types of trauma are the same for the survivors of political violence but include a high rate of criminal acts such as armed robbery, car hijacking, burglary, traumatic bereavement, rape, child abuse, and domestic violence. South Africa is a traumatized nation, and the traumatization goes on. Poverty, HIV+ status, Aids, and unemployment are enormous, especially for black and coloured people of whom approximately 40% are unemployed; for young people this figure is as high as 60%.

There is an enormous demand for trauma psychotherapy in South Africa in an empowering, healing, and preventive sense. It is imperative for the survival of the new democracy to break the circle of violence. Therapy happens under very difficult circumstances: lack of rooms, money, time, and qualified people, etc. The most traumatized, the black and coloured people, 90% of the population, live in communities far from trauma centres and practice, and close to their traditional healers called *sangomas*. One focus of psychological trauma work is collective victim empowerment in the community, if possible, in collaboration with traditional healers.

When beginning trauma therapy with a black person, you are never sure if they will be there for the next session. There is often no transport or no money for transport. Trauma therapy in this context means mostly a brief intervention against a background of many difficulties.

An event is defined as traumatic if it is overwhelming, disempowering, disconnecting, and cannot be managed psychologically by the person alone. The personal ability to symbolize has deteriorated. The person's life story is shattered and lies in pieces. Normal flexible and creative thinking is replaced by flashbacks, nightmares, avoidance, and at times, by unconsciously driven re-enactments of the event. The loss of the capacity to process meaningful events is identified as one of the key factors which influence an individual's response to trauma. Victimization results in the shattering of basic assumptions about the self and the world such as the assumption of personal invulnerability, the perception of the world as a meaningful place, and the perception of the self as positive.

To me, as a Swiss psychoanalyst, in this context it meant understanding psychoanalytically about the unconscious, transference, and abstinence, thinking systemically in family and community terms and in a culture-sensitive way,[2] and intervening with a resource-oriented, empowering approach, respecting the South African context where traumatized people are in agony and the setting is never guaranteed.

A story begins when you decide to tell it; here an attempt to combine African tradition and Western psychoanalysis.

While story-telling is of course a cultural universal, it does seem to occupy a special place in the hearts of Africans. Once upon a time and still today, families gathered around fires and listened to the stories told by old people. There were stories about brave heroes who defended their children against the dangers and cruelties of nature. These were times when children could still trust adults, when adults could explain to them why strange things happened. African story-telling is oral, part of shared beliefs and common myths. The way the stories in the communities were told and the manner in which lessons were taught, created a sense of meaning and of community in African society. There are still a lot of mostly empowering African stories actually present in the collective memory of the society.

South Africa has just left behind the "grand narrative of apartheid", a trauma-saturated collective and individual story. The achievement of consensus through dialogue has brought the country out of the apartheid era into an ambiance in which solutions can be negotiated. To some people and communities, trauma took nearly everything away. What is left is a mostly shattered story, a shattered self. So it becomes important to construct a life-story including the trauma to become "whole".

The psychoanalytic process focuses on the transformation of unconscious fantasy into rational understanding. Psychoanalysis means in this sense, to build a "meaning" which was lost by being overcharged, by convention, anxiety, shame, and guilt; by trauma. The access to the unconscious means liberation and healing. Introducing the story-telling approach underscores the centrality of the imagination, desire, and affect in the creation of personal meaning and intersubjective understanding. In South Africa it represents a connection to an old and deep cultural tradition. Story-telling is the powerful sister of dream language;

---

[2] A South African culture-sensitive approach includes: 1. nurturing the human and spiritual relationship, 2. embedded strategies, 3. a holistic approach (psyche, body, word, and expression, etc.) and, 4. quickly adapting to all kind of obstacles and difficulties.

it is about imagination. Imaginative therapies are well known and well described as resource-oriented approaches in Western trauma therapy (Reddemann, 2001).

Trauma therapy in a country like South Africa often does not follow Western therapeutic stages: 1. establishment of safety, 2. remembrance and mourning, 3. reconnection to life (as described by Herman, 1992). We can only establish relative *safety* by building inner stability and motivating self care. We have to work simultaneously on *remembrance and mourning* and *reconnecting with life* because we never know if we will see the client again. So therapy becomes a mixture of didactic (about trauma), goal directed (about self care and stability and community) and unstructured psychoanalysis whenever you can afford it.

I would like to present two case studies. They are typical in the way that they happened in the previously described unstable setting. My leading question is how we can provide an empowering process for listening, dialoguing, and containing these multi-storied lives.[3] The two cases I have chosen lasted longer than is usual.

Case study 1: Adam

With Adam, a 30-year-old coloured man, I had 12 sessions in nearly four months. He visited the trauma centre once a week for an hour.

Session 1: A shy and thin 30-year-old coloured man is sitting in front of me for the first time. I know that he is HIV+ and is recovering from tuberculosis and meningitis he had two months before. He has been unemployed for two years. He actually left his mother's home where he had a lot of problems and fights, to work as caretaker in a community centre in the coloured community where our trauma centre is situated. He needs counselling to work on his traumas and to find a way to heal psychologically and physically. "My biggest problem is my mom." He begins to tell his first story, a story of a boy, adolescent and man, who was and is very dependent on his mom. His biological father left the family when Adam was less than one year old. He grew up with mother, stepfather, and three older siblings, all from different fathers. He felt neglected by his mother. She promised him things she

---

[3]White (1998) describes this approach in his book: a life story is not one story but lots of stories in one life.

then did not do or give to him. The family atmosphere was tense, with a lot of fighting and a constant lack of money. After the session he feels exhausted.

Session 2: He begins to tell the story of his horrible 16th year. His mother was getting divorced. He longed for his biological father but could not get information of his whereabouts from his mother. A neighbour accused him of child abuse and he had to go to court but was innocent. He dropped out of school and he got a severe infection in one leg, was comatose for two weeks, and left the hospital diagnosed with HIV+. He did not know what it meant and did not ask (South Africa in 1989).

Seven years later he had an infection in his penis, was officially tested, and informed about his HIV+ status. He was deeply shocked. Life went on. He worked as a security guard, did not think about the reasons why he was infected, had different girl friends, was unhappily married for a year (to escape his mother), and has been living as a bachelor for two years.

Session 3: He begins to talk about his "second world", an imaginary world where he has a nine-year-old daughter, his child with a woman he left in the care of her aunt nine years ago. He meets her regularly and has only to sign a form to get custody of her. It is the first time he shares this secret with someone. He speaks about a warm feeling in his chest when thinking and speaking about this second world. It is good and comforting to be there and sometimes he wishes that it would become real. Three sessions, three stories; the first insights into a multi-storied life. He brings his first and second world into the transitional space of therapy. He solves the problem of his unfulfilled wishes through a vivid fantasy world. His life runs on two tracks. Does the second world give him the energy to deal with his problems in the first world, to heal, and to find work? Or does he just not want to see reality as it is?

Sessions 4 & 5: A good colleague of his from a self-help centre passed away suddenly, a woman, HIV+, same age. He is shattered. Who will be the next to die? He is sad and angry that she left him. A cousin is stabbed to death some days after. He reveals that his second world and his shyness are an avoidance of his huge aggression. He has a fist-fight with another cousin who asks him for cigarettes and money in his mother's house. Despite the conflicts he has there, he returns home daily because he feels lonely. He applied for on-the-job training in the nearby hospice for terminally ill people and was accepted. He is happy because he has something to do now. In his presentation to the group he presents himself as a bachelor and as available. But after this initial enthusiasm he does not feel well. He fears he is getting pneumonia again; it is cold, winter time and no heating in the houses. Adam misses our next meeting.

He does not have a story which moves him forward. Past and present are difficult and hard to cope with. Adam follows an old pattern: withdrawal. I insist on a next appointment. He thinks about leaving the caretaker job and returning to his mother's home and leaving the training he had begun the week previously.

Sessions 6 & 7: He was hurt by an indiscretion at the hospice: somebody informed them about his HIV+ status. He feels insupportably lonely and reacts with withdrawal, back to square one, his old pattern. Furthermore, he has changed his "second world": he found his father, who has three children, is a widower and very sick. He asks Adam to take care of his children when he dies. Adam tells this story in such a lively way that I ask him, "You found your father?"

Both second worlds have the same things in common, that he has to care for children and act in a responsible way towards other people.

Session 8: His introduction as a bachelor and available was successful. He now has a black girlfriend with a nine-year-old child. But he did not dare to inform her about his HIV+ status and put it in an imaginary box, in his "box of pain". He suggested that they both go for a test. He is scared that she will leave him when she knows that he is HIV+. Perhaps she is infected too? They already speak about having a child together. He knows that he has to tell the truth in the next weeks.

At the next meeting he does not appear. Which story will be the true one in the end?

Session 9: His girlfriend heard about his HIV+ status from another person and was devastated. Adam tried to hang himself; an attempt at total withdrawal, perhaps trying unconsciously to put outside what is inside and to accuse everybody, his girlfriend, his mother, through this act. He survived; in his words, "I tested God" and his new girlfriend. She did not dump him but took him to a traditional healer to heal him of being HIV+. They joined a religious group to pray together for his health.

Sessions 10, 11 & 12: He is happy that his girlfriend is standing by him. Despite this he thinks about returning home to his mother. He feels too lonely staying alone in his room. He says that his feelings have changed a lot over the last months. He feels stronger and he feels more independent regarding his mother, so he eventually decides to return home. He had a discussion with his mother about their relationship and he feels good about that. He now has a new perspective on his life. So we agree to close the therapy.

Case study 2: Dina

I had 15 sessions with Dina over a period of one year. We met irregularly because she often missed the sessions.

Dina is a 16-year-old refugee from Rwanda. When she was seven years old her mother was shot by the army before her eyes. With father and siblings she fled through different countries to arrive in Johannesburg six years ago. Her unemployed father is responsible for five children and is very concerned about Dina: traumatized, fainting, headaches, lack of concentration at school, lazy at home, and making bad friends, he says. He fears losing her like two of his older children during the years spent fleeing.

Session 1: She tells me the story of her alarming lack of concentration at school, her permanent headaches, dizziness, and fainting. She has a lot of fights in her daily life with her father, as she is the oldest daughter in a patriarchal household without a mother, and with her siblings in the small flat; fights about space, gossiping, lack of appreciation, and respect. When she gets angry and disappointed she bangs her head against the wall. Could this have something to do with her headache, dizziness, fainting? I ask her. Yes, it could be.

Sessions 2–7: In the following months she introduces me to her difficult story of being hurt and hurting herself. She cannot talk about it but writes it down during our sessions. She writes about cutting her toes with a knife and cutting her skull after the murder of her mother (age 7–10). She tells me about her suicide attempts over the last few years after being beaten up by her father. Once he strangled her and she hid the bruises.

We talk about alternatives to her self-destructive, acting out of her anger. We do imaginations of the safe inner place, of inner helpers and she likes to do this. I meet with her father several times to talk seriously to him and he seems to understand my concern.

She does not appear at the clinic for about half of the appointments; no money for transport, or no taxi, or simply no excuse because she does not have a phone to call me. I often feel disappointed and angry. She shows me what has happened and happens to her. One day she speaks about how she feels my anger. I try to explain it to her. She agrees with me; she can follow me. However, it happens again; she does not come and she cannot cancel because she does not have money to call; that's her life. I have to accept it. In her distress she sets the rules.

Session 8: She is terribly tired and lies down on the couch. She is sucking her thumb, telling me that today is her 16th birthday. How good that she told me. Then I ask her about the sucking and she tells me that she likes it. She does it regularly in the evening to fall asleep. She tells about a dream where somebody put wires around her teeth; it was very painful. I reply that it sounds as if she would like to stop sucking? She does not know.

Session 9: She remains at first silent and slowly begins to cry. Can she write down what she feels? She can and writes throughout the whole session. Afterwards, I read again the frightening story of being beaten up and strangled by her father, about two suicide attempts with the anti-epileptic tablets she got from the hospital and that I should keep it a secret.

Session 10: She denies everything she wrote during the last session and refuses to speak about what happened.

The therapy is stuck. She misses many sessions. I get the feeling that coming to the trauma clinic is a regressive process for her. I fantasize that I should fetch her from school and bring her here. With the accumulation of missed sessions the regression increases. Probably there is too much sadness and disappointment in her life to discuss with me. I understand her regression in therapy as the only place on earth where she can let go; in her difficult daily life, it is too dangerous to regress because she has to be strong.

I am preparing the report for the child protection unit and speak with her social worker and her father. Her father says that Dina is mad, trying to kill herself. Not mad, I reply, but desperate and it has to do with him. He tries to understand and I feel his very African values and his distress with his difficult family situation. He is a patriarch; Dina has to be responsible for cleaning and cooking and he has a right to dominate and beat her up.

I am planning a family and social worker meeting. It never happens. Dina tries to calm me. Her father asks me some days later in all seriousness to become Dina's mother and take her with me to Switzerland, a typical African request. Dina and her father are disappointed at my refusal.

Sessions 11–13: It goes up and down. Sometimes she comes to the sessions, sometimes not. Sometimes she talks, sometimes she only writes things down. Orally, she often brings her problems in a disguised form, such as saying that her best friend tried to kill herself. When she finally writes down what has happened to her, it's always a sad and horrible story.

I try to support her, listening to or reading her stories, and encouraging her to find a solution. Her relationship with her father remains difficult. The headaches and fainting are still the same. She is disappointed that her father does not care. Perhaps it would be a solution to move forward, relying on her peers.

Session 14: A new story is told, a story of pretending. At school she has been pretending for years that her father has a good job, that they are wealthy and that everything is okay. Only the teachers seem to know that she lives with a brutal and unemployed father, sharing her bed with her cousin behind a curtain in the kitchen, very busy in the household instead of doing homework for school, without money to buy the necessary school books. But she will no longer simulate a life which is not hers; she will tell the truth about her life and her worries and her lack of everything.

Session 15: It was the last session we had fixed after one year of therapy. She lost the courage and the initiative to tell the true story at school. Perhaps it is too hard, she does not know. Now she has to prepare for her final exam at school.

Discussion

Adam and Dina have both been heavily traumatized since childhood and live in ongoing traumatizing circumstances. Their therapy takes place in an unstable and irregular way. Every session becomes in a way a personal story. Their lives are also full of different stories, true ones and pretend ones.

The challenge for the therapist is to listen carefully to the manifest stories and to help the client to find the latent one; to combine the different stories into one life story, his or her life story respectively, from the multi-storied life integrating trauma.

Dina's breakdowns—beaten up, banging her head, trying to kill herself—depict a difficult story of an adolescent refugee which is still ongoing. What makes the story go on? Dina decided to tell the story and to spread it. People around her must know; she needs "communities of acknowledgement" (White, 1997) to tell and retell. A story begins when you decide to tell it. Then it is an event and to listen to it can become an act of self empowerment.

Trauma also wrote and writes Dina's life story: war, the death of her mother, flight, being a refugee, and her father beating her up. It is an ongoing traumatization. In her "pretend story" she denied the trauma to her peer group; her wish was to belong to the group, to be like the others. In her attempt to tell the true story, she is trying to tell herself into her own story, in her personal being, in her truth about how she lives. A question remains open: does the outer pressure allow her a development of the inner world?. She is pious and tries to be a good person; she is concerned and caring for other people and tries to help them.

At every session Adam tells new stories, true ones and pretend ones. He shows me his past and present life in stories and asks me if one day I could write it down because he thinks that it is a thrilling story about both of his worlds. By his asking this question, I can feel his sense of pride in his imagination; he is poor and sick, but he has a second world which is an ongoing story of his own. Eventually he takes decisions in his actual life.

Trauma wrote his life story; father left, stepfather, HIV+, many suicide attempts. In his second world, he himself is the writer. In life Adam now needs "communities of acknowledgement" where he can share his experiences of the first life. By telling me his stories he is developing new ideas about becoming more active in his life. In fact, he is a very caring person in his environment.

Dina and Adam shared their stories with me and I witnessed and acknowledged them. Both need to go forward and need resourceful stories to face their problems. They need to be the authors of their life, being in charge and focused on their resources, gently moving away from self blame, recrimination, and self judgement.

One story—multistoried life and integrating trauma

Telling the story is like weaving a mat. The mat is a metaphor for connection and disconnection. The mats are used to communicate relational ideas about commitment, family, religion, and belonging. Life is multistoried, of course. In my understanding, the different stories are the pattern on the mat and it is important to be aware of the entire mat, the entire life.

Trauma has to do with isolation, unbearable contradictions, and with splitting. As a therapist therefore, you always have to think of the opposite and of the latent content of what is said. We are empowering the client to tell and retell the story in a way that makes them stronger. Sometimes we have to clarify first in what ways trauma is weakening and disempowering a person. It is wise to do this in an empowering, resource-oriented way.

We live by the stories we have about our lives; they shape our lives.

A woman who had been hijacked twice phoned to tell me that the following day it would be a year since the second hijacking and that she had been terrified of this day for weeks. I asked her if she could perhaps celebrate being alive on that day, but she found it cynical. So I asked her to celebrate all the good things, her new stories, which had happened during this year. From the therapy sessions, I knew that there were good things.

Trauma can catch, hold, and occupy mind and body. A trauma is never one single event but the complex product of what happened before, then, and after. Story-telling describes events in a time sequence and gives the possibility to change the story. Telling the story and looking for a witness, a community of acknowledgment, means already moving the mind in another direction. It is empowering.

The way forward

A survivor has to cultivate his resources to cope with the trauma. This can be through faith, spirituality, through the imagination, an inner stage with a safe place, helpers, a pain or joy box, and by telling stories. Other resources are the family, friends, other support systems, groups, and communities. The feeling of being connected to others provides the strongest protection against terror, despair, and trauma (Hermann, 1992).

It is about remembering the past without getting stuck in it; putting the memories together again in a different way, so that one can deal with them. Maybe then, one can try to forgive and so to step out of "victimhood". Therapy ends, in the best cases, when a person decides that their self-story is rich enough to go forward. Psychoanalysis can be used to achieve this handling of unconscious, transference, setting, and abstinence; it is in the mind and heart and handling, the hands, of the therapist. Often you have to adapt it to an ongoing traumatizing context (Ley & Garcia, 2003).

Two true stories to conclude

Charlene Smith, a raped South African journalist, wrote: "They wounded my body, my psyche, but they could never touch my soul, they could never take my spirit. Today I feel no hatred towards the person who raped me, because hatred would destroy me." She had written down her story in the year after the rape and had published it together with the collected material of hundreds of women's stories about rape and Aids (Smith, 2001).

In 1996, Mr Sikwepere gave his testimony before the South African Truth and Reconciliation Commission. He had lost his eyesight at the hands of police bullets during apartheid. He told about the trauma, his terrible headaches, and finished with the words, "I feel that what has been making me sick all this time is the fact that I could not tell my story. But now—I feel like I got my sight back by coming here and telling you" (Kotzé et al., 2002).

CHAPTER NINE

The psychoanalyst: from private witness to public testimony

Andrés Gautier

The Era of the Witness

The Era of the Witness is in fact the title of a book written by the French historian Annette Wieviorka (1998), who specializes in the history of the Jewish people in the 20th century, with particular emphasis on the Holocaust and on the need to keep those events present in our mind as a historical memory. She begins her account with the words attributed to Simon Doubnov who, shortly before he was assassinated in Riga on December 8, 1941, said to those who were with him in the ghetto: "Good people, never forget; go forth and testify; write it all down!" (Vidal-Naquet, 1994, p. v). The point he was making was that these events had to be made known and that an account of them had to be passed on, whatever the price that had to be paid. He imposed on those who survived both an "obligation to remember" and a "duty to remind others".

From a psychoanalytic perspective, this process is highly significant, given that:

> *Where transgressions have been committed which endanger the very foundations of the social existence of human beings, a recollection of what has*

happened is of vital importance for the survival of any culture. In the Freudian myth of the historical origin of culture—that of the father of the primal horde and his murder—awareness of transgression is required in order to enable the foundations of society to be established.

It is only when a traumatic human experience has been made known to others that there exists an opportunity for that experience to be processed and worked through.

It is only when the perpetrator and the consequences of the act have been condemned, that there exists a possibility that the incriminated act will never be repeated.

Recent thinking about horrendous events caused by our fellow human beings has given rise to a legal concept which defines certain state-instigated crimes as crimes against humanity; this in turn has given rise to legal procedures by which those accused of such crimes may be brought to justice. One recent example is that of General Pinochet, who was arrested in Great Britain on an international warrant.

Jean-François Chiantaretto, the French psychoanalyst and author of a book (2004, p. ix) on the theme of bearing witness and trauma, high-lights the fact that in the 20th century, ever since the mass murders of the First World War, the Armenian genocide, and the Holocaust, the concept of bearing witness has taken on particular significance. Concomitantly, a revival of the debate on the treatment of people who have been trauma-tized has also taken place, and there is renewed interest in the Freudian model of trauma. It must be said though, as Gubrich-Simitis writes, Freud never fully abandoned his model of trauma (1998), although he did look upon it with some ambivalence, fearing that the "trauma model could endanger the radically new, long unwelcome, more complex, and more improbable instinct (or conflict) model" (ibid., p. 109).

Case histories as testimony

What Fritz Morgenthaler said about Freud's "interpretation of dreams" is equally true of his case histories: they result from the pressure placed on psychoanalytic theory to provide some means of verification. The issue here was how to lend weight to Freud's idea of the unconscious, of repression, etc.: "By their origin, structure and interpretability, dreams provided the evidence that the basic tenets of psychoanalysis were correct" (1986, p. 19).

Following on from Breuer's "Anna O." (1895d), Freud's own case histories represent a significant contribution to psychoanalytic theory; they both illustrate and substantiate its hypotheses. In addition to providing us with a clear picture of the psychoanalytic method, these clinically oriented contributions go a long way towards authenticating Freudian theory and technique in their wider sense. The psychoanalyst has both to facilitate and to interpret an ongoing process. Freud's case histories bear witness also to his fascination with what is possible and/ or not possible in ordinary psychoanalytic practice.

What Freud, however, failed to take into consideration was the fact that in several of his cases, he himself was being enrolled as a potential witness, as it were, to a given version of events. As Chiantaretto points out, the function of the psychoanalyst as a receptacle of testimony is an inherent dimension of the psychoanalytic process: psychoanalysis resembles a "… witness stand for the analysand, at least at certain points in the unfolding of the transference dynamics and in certain therapies" (2004, p. x).

Two examples

A pleasant-looking woman, about 70 years of age, was referred to me by her doctor. During our initial conversation, it became clear to me that the reason she wanted a consultation was that she felt she needed to reveal a family secret.

Shortly after the Second World War, when she was still a young woman, she fell in love with a young German who lived in Switzerland, and became pregnant by him. Without knowing anything about that situation, the young man returned to Germany. When her parents, who were strict Catholics, learned of their daughter's pregnancy, they cut her off from all social contact until after the baby's birth, which took place in the maternity unit of another town, so that nobody in the family's immediate environment would learn about it. The baby remained with his mother during her stay in hospital, and was thereafter placed in a home. Mother was permitted to visit her child at weekends. The infant, a child conceived in love, died in that home.

Up until the time of our conversation, that 70-year-old woman had kept this secret to herself and had never spoken of her corresponding pain and feelings of guilt. At no other point during her parents' lifetime did she discuss what had happened with them. As her sessions with me progressed, she made contact with her former German friend, by now an emeritus professor, and announced her intention to visit him. She was warmly welcomed by his family, and told him of the events about which he knew nothing: her pregnancy, the birth and subsequent death of their son. They were able to share both the distress and the joy of the time they had spent together so many years before. During our conversations, other family secrets were revealed. After eight sessions, she took leave of me, thanking me warmly for my help. in a way that she felt was satisfactory, she had been able to have closure on something of significant importance for her.

My second example is Freud's case study of Katharina, taken from *Studies on Hysteria* (1895). Freud recounts that he was on vacation, trying to forget about neuroses for a while. During a walk in the mountains, while he was taking a rest on the summit, he was approached by someone who asked him if he was indeed a doctor. The person turned out to be the young woman of about 18 who had served him lunch. She told Freud that she was suffering from a nervous condition and that the medical treatment she had was of no help. What was Freud's reaction? Even though he was on holiday, his curiosity was awakened: "I was interested to find that neuroses could flourish in this way at a height of over 6,000 feet; I questioned her further therefore" (ibid., p. 125).

To begin with, Katharina described her somatic complaints, which Freud saw as being symptomatic of anxiety. Then he asked her: "When you have an attack, do you think of something? And always the same thing? Or do you see something in front of you?" (ibid., p. 126). Katharina replied: "Yes. I always see an awful face that looks at me in a dreadful way, so that I'm frightened" (ibid., p. 126). When asked at what point she first began having these visions, she replied: "Two years ago." Then Freud tried what he himself called "a lucky guess": "At that time [...] you must have seen or heard something that very much embarrassed you, and that you'd much rather not have seen" (ibid., p. 127). Thereupon, Katharina confirmed Freud's supposition: "Heavens, yes!" she replied, "That was when I caught my uncle with the girl, with Franziska, my cousin" (ibid., p. 127). Freud then simply helped her describe the experience. Whenever he intervened, his aim was to understand and to establish connections regarding the possible meaning of that hideous face with its fear-inspiring eyes. In the course of her narrative, Katharina reported two occurrences that had taken place two or three years prior to the traumatic event already mentioned. The first was when her uncle had tried to molest her sexually as she was lying in bed. The second was when her uncle, completely drunk, once again tried to harass her. As she finished recounting these memories, Freud observed that: "[She] was like someone transformed. The sulky, unhappy face had grown lively, her eyes were bright, she was lightened and exalted" (ibid., p. 131). Freud then made an interpretation that linked these various, apparently isolated, memories together: "I know now what it was you thought when you looked into the room. You thought: 'Now he's doing with her what he wanted to do with me that night and those other times.' That was what you were disgusted at, because you remembered that feeling you had when you woke up in the night and felt his body" (ibid., p. 131). In concluding his report, Freud again turns to the awful look on the man's face that caused Katharina to go into a panic. She herself was then able to suggest that it was related to the hate-filled look on her uncle's face after she had discovered the sexual relationship between him and Franziska, and had informed her aunt about it. She was thus afraid that he might maltreat her. She told Freud that in the meantime her aunt had divorced her uncle. Freud ends his description of the case with the following remark: "I hope this girl, whose sexual sensibility had been injured at such an early age, derived some benefit from our conversation. I have not seen her since" (ibid., p. 133).

Freud's function in this case was that of an understanding witness who, by asking appropriate questions and creating relevant connections, made it possible for Katharina to process what she had been through and thus to gain some control over her traumatic experience.

Where a person suffers from intra-psychic conflict, he or she usually wants this resolved, while in the case of ordeals or trauma that are the consequence of external circumstances, the individual is primarily seeking the opportunity to put words to the experience and thereby find relief. This release, as it were, takes place not only through the analytical process, but also in the act of involving the perpetrator in what could be called a social act. The analyst plays the part of a first or test witness. He or she becomes society's representative, acknowledging that the analysand's story can be communicated. It is undoubtedly the case that in some situations, this corresponds to the analysand's tacit desire to have his or her story or case description published and to have the analyst agree to take on this task.

My reasoning here is in complete accord with that of Chiantaretto, the author of the outstanding work *Témoignage et Trauma* ("Testimony and Trauma", 2004), in claiming that not only is it crucial for the psychoanalytic process to acknowledge and respect as such the phases in which being a witness is paramount, but also, as Waintrater (2004) has argued, that taking on board a testimony of this kind is an integral part of the psychoanalytic process. This is what Waintrater has to say on the topic: "If one considers psychoanalysis as an opportunity to take in and transform emotional and mental states, there can be no doubt that testimony is somehow linked to the psychoanalytic act of listening" (2004, pp. 65–66). In other words, the analyst can help the witness, by virtue of his or her active listening and process-oriented insight, to initiate a process of coming to terms with the specific event, thus enabling that person to work through the thoughts that pour into his or her mind in a more conscious, clear, and unconstrained manner.

Although sharing one's testimony with an analyst is not psychotherapy as such, it may still have a therapeutic effect. As Waintrater puts it: "When the individual begins to speak, his or her desire is both to affirm the overwhelming aspect of the experience and to re-establish contact with mankind, with fellow human beings. The testimony thus represents an attempt to re-create some type of link at the point where the break took place" (ibid., p. 67).

In her work with witnesses, Waintrater (2004) refers to a "testimonial pact" or witnessing agreement. What does she mean by this?

> The significance of the testimony is the fact that it enables the witness to liberate him- or herself from the actual story ... The object of the testimony transmitted is therefore not what has been repressed, but rather the manifest narrative the unfolding of which is co-determined by the testimony-receiver. As an actual partner in the discussion, the analyst's presence serves as a support for the witness telling his or her story. This role, however, is different from that of a classical analyst in that the function here is not to identify the unconscious elements in the narrative of the other party to the discussion. The observations which the analyst will be able to make from them constitute an "addition" to the testimony, an added element which the analyst is obliged to keep to him- or herself, carefully refraining from making any interpretation. Too many witnesses have felt offended by interpretative listening, claiming that they had not been listened to in a manner that they felt was necessary for them (2004, p. 75).

In this agreement or pact, the position of the analyst as the receptacle of a given testimony is complicated by the fact that the expectations which he or she is supposed to live up to are often quite complex. Within the narrative process, Waintrater (2004) puts the analyst in a position similar to Bion's (1970) alpha-function: like a mother adapting to the needs of her infant, the analyst adjusts to the needs of the witness through a support function that generates meaning, while constantly remaining in tune with the psychic needs of the other person (Waintrater, 2004).

Like the analyst, the testimony-receiver, to use Waintrater's (2004) term, plays a "third-party" role; it is this that enables dialogue to take place. The capacity to negotiate between proximity and distance makes him, or her, a suitable partner in the discussion.

The private place of the clinic and the public forum of the testimony

What happens however, if the analyst becomes witness to the consequences of a "man-made catastrophe" such as torture, concentration camps, or other forms of state violence? Is it enough for him to treat such cases as though the trauma were strictly individual? Of course, it is important to treat trauma in its individual manifestations as every analyst has been trained to do, or at least should have been. The question, however, emerges as to whether or not psychoanalysts have been further invested with the inherent function of publicly co-denouncing the damage to which they have become witness.

Many authors have pointed out that it is no coincidence that the issue of trauma comes up in psychoanalytic thought and therapeutic practice in periods of brutal social violence such as, for instance, when there have been mass murders: the two World Wars, the Holocaust, the Vietnam War, and the period of state terrorism in Latin America. The psychoanalyst becomes witness to the devastating psychological repercussions of the trauma and to its effects on entire families through successive generations: violence, depression, destructive secrets, panic reactions, isolation, broken families, and children in trouble. This kind of violence has an impact that goes far beyond the oppressors and their immediate victims; it casts a shadow over the whole life of the individual, of his or her family, and of the society of which he or she is part.

When analysts are confronted with cultural transgressions which endanger, in its basic principles, the very fabric of social coexistence, are they justified in acting as though they were emissaries from the Red Cross and refrain from making any direct response within the context of that society? Parin sums up the question as follows: "Why wait until the worst has come to pass? Why not proceed, from a psychoanalytic viewpoint, to throw light on relationships of alienating work, of undesired pregnancies, and of everyday 'basic misery'? Why do the Analytical Societies remain silent, why do the real experts of our science not take Hartmann's warning to heart and open their eyes to 'the role which the economic or social structures [...] play'?" (Parin, 1978, p. 10).

That psychoanalysis can be both relevant to and interested in social issues was emphasized by Freud in his article "'Civilized' Sexual Morality and Modern Nervous Illness" (1908) and in *Totem and Taboo* (1913) in which he unambiguously states that position. In the words of Freud's biographer Rodrigué: "In *Totem and Taboo*, Freud, through confronting instinct with culture, takes a stand on behalf of the latter, especially as regards his reflections on the myth of the primal horde that he portrayed. When choosing between the unconstrained, powerful, and compulsive father of the primal horde and the guilt-ridden band of brothers seeking to create law, Freud opts for the latter, for the law and against drive-related impulse" (Rodrigué, 1996, p. 68).

Freud provides us with guidelines also with respect to the methodology we can adopt in our quest for answers: he clearly separates clinical practice from socially oriented undertakings, while nonetheless developing both of them simultaneously and consistently in his published work. *Totem and Taboo* makes ample use of vignettes, but the persons concerned are impossible to identify on a personal level. The devastated intimacy of those involved must be protected at all costs. At the same time, it can be meaningful for those affected by torture and state violence to be offered a space in which they can act as witnesses, a space quite distinct from the therapeutic setting, one in which there is a real possibility for them to express themselves in public.

The pensioners and retired workers of Bolivia demonstrate

When the Institute for Therapy and Research on Torture and State Violence (ITEI) in Bolivia launched its research activities and interviewed witnesses from among the peasants who had been victims of state violence in the year 2000, it was vitally important for those victims to be able to testify and formulate their accusations, putting words to what that brutal repression had meant for them, even if they did not want their names to be mentioned:

> We did not file any accusations, because we were frightened; at the same time, I heard that you had come here so that we could make sworn statements (Bravo, 2003, p. 125).

The ITEI took on the task of drafting a document for publication in which the events and their consequences would be portrayed. A power of attorney was set up with the obligation that it be subsequently given back, by those to whom it had been delegated, to those who were directly involved, as exemplified in the way one of the witnesses ended his comment: "… so that we can denounce what happened" (ibid.). In essence, this was a temporary delegation. The end product, i.e., the published report, was there to enable the victims to take back what quite properly belonged to them.

In January 2003, when more than 10,000 pensioners were marching towards La Paz, a distance of more than 100 km, in order to protest against a reduction in their already meagre pension allowance, they were set upon at 2 a.m. by young policemen and soldiers, young enough to be their grandchildren, in a "pre-dawn swoop". The elderly pensioners were, to all intents and purposes, abducted and taken back, manu military, to their home towns in buses to prevent them reaching La Paz. The police raid met with strong resistance on the part of the pensioners, who were forced with incredible brutality to clamber into the buses. Many of them managed to flee; still others found places to hide, with the result that early the next day, more determined than ever, the pensioners once again resumed their march. Many of those who had been abducted returned by bus the following day in order to rejoin the demonstration. The pensioners were welcomed in triumph by a large turn-out of the population of El Alto and La Paz. Emma Bolshia Bravo, ITEI's research convenor, proposed that the ITEI working group record a certain number of testimonies, while the pensioners were still in La Paz, with the aim of gathering material for a report which would later be published. As the ITEI group was conducting the interviews, a 78-year-old pensioner responded with the following remark:

> I am delighted that this testimony can be given. The fact is that we had no opportunity to express ourselves; yet at times, this type of

possibility does make itself available to us and lets us speak out and tell the truth about our pain and suffering, thereby permitting the people of Bolivia and the international community to learn that this country is indeed going through an extremely critical period (ibid., p. 119).

Arguably the most fundamental aspect of the testimonies recorded, which denounce the repression carried out by the state apparatus, was the Oedipal transgression.

Several witnesses spoke with deep indignation about the humiliation they suffered in the early morning raid of January 15 and in particular the loss of respect for people old enough to be their fathers or mothers, as this mine-leader explains:

> ... they began to pull at our comrades, male and female, dragging them along and grabbing them by their feet and their hands so as to load them into the vehicles ... They showed no respect for age, or towards the poor old defenceless women who could only cry and shout in despair. We asked them to show a little consideration, saying that they also had mothers and that they were born of women and so for that reason if for no other they should show some consideration ... Shouting at the women made them frightened ... all they wanted was some degree of justice and to be treated better (ibid., p. 129).

Their humiliation and helplessness led the women to call into question the sensitivity of those soldiers, but all that they received in response was violence. As Tisseron (1992, p. 59) puts it, for any human being who can still hold on to a modicum of self-respect, "humiliation is the worst of ordeals". The reaction to that repression was one not only of rage, impotence, suffering and pain, but also of strength and courage.

The deciding factor in this social conflict was that the demonstrators refused to take on board any feelings of shame when they saw how their elderly comrades were being treated; moreover, they made those who were in fact responsible confront those feelings. As the demonstrators managed to overcome the humiliation they suffered, a particularly significant event occurred in the attempt to put those feelings of shame back to where they should have been experienced.

Faced with the brutal intervention of the police, Mrs Segundina, the widow of a miner and a miner herself, took off all the clothing from the upper part of her body. That created an unexpected situation for the forces of law and order; the counter-attack, as it were, took the aggressors by surprise. How were they, in all conscience, to reconcile what they were doing with the fact that they too were once children, children with mothers, women who gave them life? Through her action, Mrs Segundina made the police officers face up to the depths of human degradation to which they had sunk through their attacks on the elderly.

Her undressing revealed the complete loss of moral limits in the police force:

> The soldiers then wanted to drag me away. So I took off my dress. I was only in my underskirt, nothing else except for my underwear. Then I said "What more do you want? Take me away! This is what your mother is like, this is where you came from. It is thanks to this that you grew. It is because of this that you are a soldier now, this is what you suckled." That is what I said to them, "Take me away!" The other soldier started pleading, "Madam put your clothes on …." "I'm not going to get dressed, if you want to, take me away." That's what I said to him, but nobody dared take me away, so the women stayed … (Bravo, 2003, p. 151).

Mrs Segundina reveals in her testimony that, after seeing the soldiers so emotionally distressed, the deputy minister of defence ordered women police officers to intervene. They were not at all impressed by the nakedness of the elderly women and they acted in consequence. Nevertheless, there was that defining moment when it was possible to make the transgressors face up to feelings of shame. Since in the interviews we have not found any sign of trauma, it is very probable that when confronted with such fierce repression, the retired and the elderly had the capacity to react, to put into words what happened, and to make the whole experience meaningful. More convinced than ever of their rights, they took to the streets of La Paz to further their demands.

What occurred involved transgression: the transgression of fundamental human values, and an Oedipal form of transgression at that. This was no individual phenomenon; it was that of a society in which a minister of a democratically elected government ordered his officials to infringe one of the fundamental precepts of modern civilization: to show respect, in particular towards a person old enough to be the aggressor's father or mother. A theme that has emerged from the testimonies is that there exists a feeling of deep disquiet: some young members of the police and armed forces can apparently be ordered to show a complete lack of consideration towards the elderly and in particular towards those, the elderly women, who could represent the mothers who gave them life. That is why the demonstrators asked them: "You yourself did not come from a woman, perhaps? Is that why you're showing no respect towards us?".

In Freud's (1913) myth of the primal horde, an essential moment for the very basis of human society occurs when the crime against the father is acknowledged to be a fundamental social violation and the Oedipal desire for the mother is repressed. This creates a hiatus in the repetitive mechanism of domination of the all-powerful, violent, and tyrannical father of the primal horde and lies at "the source of our morality". In the March for Survival, the part of the creators of this culture was played by women, just as was the case of the Mothers of the Plaza de Mayo in Argentina. At one point they were called "the crazy women of the Plaza de Mayo", who demanded news of their sons and daughters, nieces and nephews, granddaughters and grandsons, or husbands who "disappeared" during the military dictatorship. In our study it was also women who played a crucial role in denouncing the absence of law.

By setting soldiers and police against the elderly, the government played the part of the father of the primal horde, inciting its officials to moral perversion.

As we explore in this study how the state collapsed into barbarism, we find ourselves confronted by a transcendental phenomenon: the elderly in modern society tend to lose the place they once held within family and social structures. Through their March for Survival, they were here seen to be figures of identification and admiration, carrying upon their shoulders the long history of struggle for, and defence of, human rights.

Conclusion

As Waintrater (2004) argues, the locus in which a testimony is made is, or should become, a space in which psychoanalysts can move from witnessing in private to expressing in public; empowered to analyse, from a psychoanalytic perspective, state transgressions which endanger humanity: they can therefore denounce them. They must on the one hand take on board the testimony shared with them, and on the other, if necessary, be the instigators of a written account of that testimony. Psychoanalysts are faced with a challenge not only at the moment of the actual interview, but also regarding how to process that testimony in written form. The challenge in reproducing the testimony in book form pertains to whether or not the person who provided the testimony feels able to identify with it. At the time the book *La Represión de la Marcha por la Sobrevivencia* (The Repression of the March for Survival) was published, ITEI members travelled to many of the pensioners' home towns in order to present the book to them. It became apparent that the pensioners felt they had been empowered to reveal something of their experience in the book, and thereby to make it their own.

To put it in general terms, by virtue of becoming the receptacles of testimony, analysts find that in many cases they are simultaneously entrusted, implicitly or explicitly, with the task of ensuring that that testimony does not remain a private issue. Given this situation, analysts have several options at their disposal: if a particular witness is to any real extent able to "go public" him- or herself with the testimony, or if he or she indicates that there is a real possibility of so doing, the analyst can leave that task in the witness's hands. If, on the other hand, the testimony is an integral part of a research project, the analyst must take that task on board. Quite often, however, in actual practice, the testimony lies dormant in some zone or other of oblivion.

Both witness and analyst are called upon to share the daunting task of seeing through to completion, a society-oriented undertaking that is designed to heal the traumatic wounds. As Waintrater states in this connection: "… this is furthermore the only means by which society can be prevented from giving itself up entirely to murder" (2004, p. 68). We could say that research is one of the preferred means, but not the only one, by which analysts can carry out their task in a public forum.

To summarize, in working with the testimonies of those who are victims of state violence for political reasons, the psychoanalyst becomes the privileged witness to a narrative that is both personal and public, one which is often traumatic, one which cries out for public expression, disclosure, and accusation. In this situation, the psychoanalyst becomes a possible fellow combatant in the struggle against barbarism.

REFERENCES

Adelman, A. (1995). Traumatic memory and the intergenerational transmission of Holocaust narratives. *Psychoanalytic Study of the Child*, *50*: 343–367.

Agger, I. (1992). *The Blue Room*. London: Zed.

Almqvist, K. & Broberg, A. G. (1997). Silence and survival: working with strategies of denial in families of traumatised pre-school children. *Journal of Child Psychotherapy*, *23*(3): 417–435.

Amati Sas, S. (1977). Qualche riflessione sulla tortura per introdurre una discussione psicoanalitica. *Rivista di Psicoanalisi*, *23*: 3. Published as *Thoughts on torture*. London: Free Association, 1988.

Amati Sas, S. (1989). Recupérer la honte. In: J. Puget, R. Käes et al. (Eds.), *Violence d'Etat et Psychoanalyse*. Paris: Dunod; *Violenza di Stato e Psicoanalisi*. Naples: Gnocchi.

Amati Sas, S. (1992). Ambiguity as the route to shame. *International Journal of Psychoanalysis*, *73*: 329–334.

Amati Sas, S. (1992a). Ethics, shame and countertransference. *Psychoanalytic Inquiry*, *12*: 570–579.

Amati Sas, S. (1994). Etica e Trans-soggettività. *Rivista di Psicoanalisi*: XL.

Amati Sas, S. (2000). La interpretación en el transubjectivo. *Revista de Psicoanálisis*, Buenos Aires, 1.

Amati Sas, S. (2004). Traumatic social violence: Challenging our unconscious adaptation. *International Forum of Psychoanalysis*, 13: 51–59.

Anzieu, D. (1984). *The Group and the Unconscious*. London: Routledge & Kegan Paul.

Arnaud, G. (2003). *Money as Signifier*. London: Free Association.

Aulagnier, P. (1979). *Les destins du plaisir. Aliénation-amour-passion*. Paris: PUF.

Berenstein, I. (2001). The link and the other. *International Journal of Psychoanalysis*, 82: 141.

Bettelheim, B. (1952). *Surviving and other essays*. New York: Alfred Knopf.

Bion, W. R. (1957). On arrogance. In: *Second Thoughts* (pp. 86–92). London: Karnac, 1993.

Bion, W. R. (1963). *Elements of Psycho-Analysis*. London: Karnac, 1984.

Bion, W. R. (1965). *Transformations*. London: Karnac, 1984.

Bion, W. R. (1967). Notes on memory and desire. In: *Cogitations*. London: Karnac, 1992.

Bion, W. R. (1970). *Attention and Interpretation*. London: Karnac, 1984.

Blackwell, D. (2005). *Counselling and Psychotherapy with Refugees*. London: Jessica Kingsley.

Blass, R. B. & Blatt, S. J. (1992). Attachment and separateness: a theoretical context for the integration of object relations theory with self psychology. *The Psychoanalytic Study of the Child*, 47: 189–204.

Bleger, J. (1967). *Simbiosis y ambigedad, estudio psicoanlítico*. Buenos Aires: Editorial Paidós.

Bleger, J. (1987). Le groupe comme institution et le groupe dans les institutions. In: R. Kaes (Ed.), *L'institution et les institutions*. Paris: Dunod, Parislista.

Blos, P. (1989). *The Adolescent Passage: Developmental Issues*. Madison, CT: International Universities Press.

Bollas, C. (1992). The Fascist state of mind. In: *Being a Character, Psychoanalysis of Self Experience* (pp. 193–217). London: Routledge.

Bollas, C. (1999). *The Return of the Oppressed*. Unpublished paper. Also in: Occasional madness of the psychoanalyst. In: *The Mystery of Things* (pp. 140–148). London: Routledge.

Borgogno, F. (2003). *Ferenczi oggi*. Turin: Bollati Boringhieri.

Bravo, E. B. (Dir.) (2003). *La Represión de la Marcha por la Sobrevivencia. Estudios sobre las secuelas psicosociales de la Violencia Estatal*. La Paz: Instituto de Terapia e Investigación sobre las Secuelas de la Tortura y violencia Estatal.

Britton, R. (2005). *Endogenous Trauma and Psychophobia*. Paper presented at International Psycho-Analytical Association Congress in Rio de Janeiro.

Campbell, J. (1978). *Le livre du Héros*. Paris: Fayard.

Castillo, R. J. (1996). *Culture and Mental Illness: A Client-Centered Approach*. Pacific Grove, CA: Brooks/Cole.

Centre of the Study of Violence and Reconciliation (1999). *Victim Empowerment and Trauma Support Work. A Training Programme*. Johannesburg: CSVR.

Chiantaretto, F. (Ed.) (2004). *Témoignage et trauma—implications psychanalytiques*. Paris: Dunod.

Clair, J. (1989). *Méduse*. Paris: Gallimard.

Clerc, D. (2000). *La Monnaie, un Vecteur du Lien Social*, quoted by Arnaud, Gilles. London: Free Association.

Danieli, Y. (1981). Differing adaptational styles in families of survivors of the Nazi Holocaust. *Children Today*, Sept.–Oct.: 6–10, 34–35.

Danieli, Y. (1984). Psychotherapists' participation in the conspiracy of silence about the Holocaust. *Psychoanalytic Psychology*, 1(1): 23–42.

Devereux, G. (1983). *Baubo, la vulve mythique*. Paris: Jean-Cyrille Godefroy.

Dumezil, G. (1969). *The Destiny of the Warrior*. Chicago: University of Chicago Press.

Dumezil, G. (1973). *Gods of the Ancient Northmen*. Los Angeles: University of California Press.

Eigen, M. (1985). Towards Bion's starting point: between catastrophe and faith. *International Journal of Psychoanalysis*, 66: 321–330.

Eigen, M. (1999). *Toxic Nourishment*. London: Karnac.

Ferenczi, S. (1923). Symbolisme de la tête de méduse et autres textes. *Internationale Zeitschrift für Psychoanalyse*, Vienna, IX: 68–70.

Ferenczi, S. (1932). Confusione delle lingue tra adulti e bambini. In: *Fondamenti della psicoanalisi*, Vol. 3 (1974), Rimini: Guaraldi.

Ferenczi, S. (1982). Confusion de langue entre les adultes et l'enfant. In: *Psychoanalyse IV, OEuvres complètes 1927–1933*. Paris: Payot.

Ferenczi, S. (1985). *Journal Clinique Janvier-Octobre 1932*. Paris: Payot.

Ferenczi, S. (1988). *The Clinical Diary of Sándor Ferenczi*. M. Balint & N. Zarday Jackson (Trans.). Cambridge, MA: Harvard University Press, 1932.

Fleury, F. (1995). C'est la barak a qui m'a sorti d'affaire. *2e Colloque européen, Migration Santé*, N° 81/82.

Fleury, F. & Gafner, N. (2000). *The Emergence of Gathering Mechanisms among Exiled Bosnian War Widows living in Switzerland*. Challenges for Public Health at the Dawn of the 21st Century, pp. 154–156, 9th International Congress of the WFPHA, Beijing, 2000.

Fleury, F. & Gillard, D. (1998). Le malheur est tombé sur le toit de la maison. *Émergence des ressources avec des familles en exil*. Geneva: IES.

Foulkes, S. H. & Anthony, E. J. (1990). *Group Psychotherapy—the Psychoanalytic Approach*. London: Maresfield Library.

Freud, A. (1936). *The Ego and the Mechanisms of Defense*, New York: International Universities Press.

Freud, S. (1900). *Drømmetydning: II.* Copenhagen: Hans Reitzel 1960 (*The Interpretation of Dreams* (3rd edition). Chapter VII. The Psychology of the dream processes. E. The primary and secondary processes. Repression. Standard Edition IV–V/*Die Traumdeutung*. Gesammelte Werke II–III).

Freud, S. (1913). Totem and Taboo. *S. E., 13*. London: Hogarth.

Freud, S. (1917). Fiksering til traumet. Det ubevidste. 18. forelæsning. I: *Psykoanalyse. Samlede Forelæsninger* (pp. 210–220). Copenhagen: Hans Reitzel, 1990. (*Vorlesungen zur einführung in die Psychoanalyse*. Gesammelte Werke XI; Standard Edition XV–XVI).

Freud, S. (1917–1923). Introduction to the book: "Psicoanalisi delle nevrosi di guerra". In: *Freud Opere 1917–1923 volume 9*. Turin: Paolo Boringhieri, 1977.

Freud, S. (1919). *Il perturbante*. O.S.F., Vol. 9, 81–114.

Freud, S. (1920). *Hinsides lystprincippet. Metapsykologi 2*. Copenhagen: Hans Reitzel, 1983. (*Jenseits des Lustprinzips*. Gesammelte Werke XIII; Standard Edition XVIII).

Freud, S. (1921). *Psicologia delle masse e analisi dell'Io*. Turin: Biblioteca Boringhieri, 1975.

Freud, S. (1922). *La tête de Méduse*. In Résultats, idées, problèmes II, pp. 49–50. Paris: PUF, 1985.

Freud, S. (1923). *The Ego and the Id. S. E., 19*. London: Hogarth.

Freud, S. (1924). Nevrosi e psicosi. In *"Collected papers"*, Vol. II. London: Hogarth.

Freud, S. (1929). *Civilization and its Discontents. S. E., 21*. London: Hogarth.

Freud, S. & Breuer, J. (1895d). *Studies on Hysteria. S. E., 2*. London: Hogarth.

Gaensbauer, T. J. (1995). Trauma in the preverbal period: symptoms, memories and developmental impact. *Psychoanalytic Study of the Child, 50*: 123–149.

Gampel, Y. (2000). Reflections on the prevalence of the uncanny in social violence. In: A. Robben & O. Suarez-Orozoo (Eds.), *Cultures under Siege: Collective Violence and Trauma in Interdisciplinary Perspectives*. Cambridge: Cambridge University Press.

Garbarino, J. & Kostelny, K. (1996). What do we need to know to understand children in war and community violence? In: R. J. Apfel & B. Simon (Eds.), *Minefields in their Hearts: The Mental Health of Children in War and Communal Violence* (pp. 33–51). New Haven, CT: Yale University Press.

Garland, C. (1998). *Understanding Trauma. A Psychoanalytical Approach*. London: Duckworth.

Godard, M. O. (2003). *Rêves et traumatismes*, Ramonville St Agne, France: Editions Erès.

Graessner, S., Gurris, N. & Pross, C. (Eds.) (2001). *At the Side of Torture Survivors*. Baltimore, MD: Johns Hopkins University Press.

Gressot, M. (1966). *L'interdit de l'inceste, précurseur et noyau du Surmoi Oedipien*. Revue française de psychanalyse, Congrès Langues Romanes.

Grimal, P. (1951). *Dictionnaire de la mythologie grecque et romaine*. Paris: PUF.

Grubrich-Simitis, I. (1981). Extreme traumatization as cumulative trauma: Psychoanalytical investigations of the effects of concentration camps on survivors and their children. *Psychoanalytic Study of the Child, 36*: 415–450.

Grubrich-Simitis, I. (1998). Es war nicht der "Sturz aller Werte". In: A.-M. Schlösser & K. Höhfeld (Eds.), *Trauma und Konflikt* (pp. 97–112). Giessen, Germany: Psychosozial-Verlag.

Grünbaum, L. (2000). Líncubo post-traumatico: via regia alla cura inconscia della scissione traumatica? *Richard e Piggle, 2*: 181–190.

Grünbaum, L. (2001). Det posttraumatiske mareridt—En vej til integration. *Matrix, 1–2*: 29–56.

Grünbaum, L. (2005). Supervision af børnepsykoterapi—overvejelser om den kulturelle og samfundsmæssige kontekst. *Matrix, 4*: 438–454.

Grünbaum, L. (2007). Supervision ved tværkulturelle problemstillinger. In: C. Haugaard Jacobsen & K. V. Mortensen: *Psychodynamisk Supervision—Teori og Praksis*. Copenhagen: Akademisk forlag.

Haynal, A., Molnar, M. & Depuymege, G. (1980). *Le fanatisme: Histoire et psychanalyse*. Paris: Stock.

Hermann, L. J. (1992). *Trauma and Recovery*. New York: Basic Books and London: Pandora, 1997.

Hollander, L. M. (Trans.) (1962). *The Poetic Edda*. Austin, TX: University of Texas Press, 1986.

Houseman, M. (1986). Le mal pour le mâle: Un bien initiatique. In: *Le mal et la douleur*. Neuchâtel, Switzerland: Musée d'ethnographie.

Jung, C. G. & Kerenyi, K. (1992). *Essays on a Science of Mythology*. New York: Pantheon, 1949.

Jung, C. G., Kereny, C. & Del Medico, H. E. (1993). *Introduction à l'essence de la mythologie: L'enfant divin, la jeune fille divine*. Paris: Payot.

Kohut, H. (1966). Forms and transformation of narcissism. *Journal of the American Psychoanalytic Association, 14*: 243–272.

Kohut, H. (1971). *The Analysis of the Self*. New York: International Universities Press.

Kohut, H. (1972). Thoughts on narcissism and narcissistic rage. In: *The Psychoanalytic Study of the Child, 27*: 360–400.

Kohut, H. (1984). *How does Analysis Cure?* In: A. Goldberg & P. Stepansky (Eds.). Chicago: University of Chicago Press.

Kohut, H. (1991). *The Search for the Self. Selected Writings of Heinz Kohut, 1950–1978*. P. Ornstein (Ed.). New York: International Universities Press.

Kotzé, E., Kotzé D., et al. (2002) Ubuntu: Caring for people and community in South Africa. In: *The International Journal of Narrative Therapy and Community Work*. Adelaide, Australia.

Krystal, H. (1971). Review of the findings and implications of this symposium. In: H. Krystal & W. G. Niederland (Eds.), *Psychic Traumatization*. Boston: International Psychiatry Clinics, *8*(1): 217–229.

Krystal, H. & Niederland, W. G. (1968). Clinical observations on the survivor syndrome. In: H. Krystal (Ed.), *Massive Psychic Trauma*. New York: International Universities Press.

Lachal, C., et al. (2003). *Comprendre et soigner le trauma en situation humanitaire*. Paris: Dunod (Collection Psychothérapies).

Ladame, F. (1995). The importance of dreams and action in the adolescent process. *International Journal of Psychoanalysis, 76*(6): 1143–1154.

Lansky, M. R. & Bley, C. R. (1995). *Posttraumatic Nightmares: Psychodynamic Explorations*. Hillsdale, NJ: The Analytic Press.

Laplanche, J. & Pontalis, J. B. (1993). Enciclopedia della psicoanalisi. Bari-Rome: Laterza.

Laub, D. & Auerhahn, N. C. (1993). Knowing and not knowing. Massive psychic trauma: Forms of traumatic memory. *International Journal of Psychoanalysis, 74*: 287–302.

Lecouteaux, C. (1999). *Chasses fantastiques et cohortes de la nuit au Moyen Âge*. Paris: Imago.

Ley, K. & Garcia, M. (2003). Psychological and moral support work with refugee women. *AGENDA. Empowering women for gender equity, 55*: 53–59, Durban.

Ley, K. & Karrer, C. (2004). *Überlebenskünstlerinnen. Frauen in Südafrika*. Bern, Switzerland: eFeF Verlag.

Lira, E. & Weinstein, E. (1984). *Psicoterapia y Represión Política*. Mexico: Siglo Veintiuno Editores.

Mahler, M. S., Pine, F. & Bergman, A. (1975). *The Psychological Birth of the Human Infant*. New York: Basic.

Mann, G. (2002). Between transformation and termination: Links in the therapeutic field and beyond. In: E. Perroni (Ed.), *The Play*, Tel Aviv: Yediot Achronot Books (in Hebrew).

Mann, G. (2007). Emotional blindness and its transformation. *The Psychoanalytic Review, 94*(2): 291–313.

Matte Blanco, I. (1975). *The Unconscious as Infinite Sets*. London: Duckworth.

Matte Blanco, I. (1988). *Thinking, Feeling and Being*. London and New York: Routledge and The Institute of Psycho-Analysis.

Métraux, J. C. (2004). *Deuils collectifs et création sociale*. Paris: Editions La Dispute.

Morgenthaler, F. (1986). *Der Traum*. Frankfurt am Main, Germany: Edition Qumran.

Niederland, W. G. (1967). Clinical observations on the survivor syndrome. *International Journal of Psychoanalysis, 49*: 313–315.

Niederland, W. G. (1986). The survivor syndrome: further observations and dimensions. *Journal of the American Psychoanalytical Association, 29*(2): 413–425.

Oury, J. (1991). L'horreur: Thèmes et variations. In: Horreur, *Revue de Médecine Psychosomatique, 28*.

Parin, P. (1978). Warum die Psychoanalytiker so ungern zu brennenden Zeitproblemen Stellung nehmen. Eine ethnologische Betrachtung. In: *Der Widerspruch im Subjekt—Ethnopsychoanalytische Studien* (pp. 7–19), Frankfurt am Main, Germany: Syndikat.

Parin, P. (1983). Die Angst der Mächtigen vor öffentlicher Trauer. In: *Subjekt im Widerspruch*. Frankfurt am Main, Germany: Syndicat, 1986.

Puget, J. (1989). In: J. Puget, R. Kaës, et al. (Eds.) *Violence d'État et Psychanalyse*. Paris: Dunod. Italian translation: *Violenza di Stato e Psicoanalisi*. Naples: Gnocchi Editore, 1994.

Puget, J. (1995). Psychic reality or various realities. *International Journal of Psychoanalsis, 76*: 29–34.

Rabanal, C. R. (1995). *Elend und Gewalt. Eine psychoanalytische Studie aus Peru*. Frankfurt, Germany: Fischer.

Rachlin, R. & Rachlin, I. (1990). *16 år i Sibirien; Skæbner i Sibirien* [2. Udgave]. Copenhagen: Gyldendal, 2000.

Reddemann, L. (2001). *Imagination als heilsame Kraft. Psychodynamic Imaginative Psychotherapie of Trauma*. Stuttgart, Germany: Pfeiffer bei Clett-Cotta. (English translation script available from Katharina Ley.)

Reyes, A. (1989). The destruction of the soul: a treatable disease? *British Journal of Psychotherapy, 6*(2).

Reyes, A., Reyes, P. & Skelton, R. (1997). Traumatized logic: the containing function of unconscious classification in the aftermath of extreme trauma. *J. M. Klein & Object Relations, 10*(4).

Ricoeur, P. (1988). L'identité narrative. In: S. Bonzon et al. (Eds.), *La Narration: Quand le récit devient communication*. Geneva: Labor et Fides (Lieux Théologiques N°. 12).

Rodrigué, E. (1996). *Sigmund Freud—El Siglo del Psicoanálisis*. Buenos Aires: Editorial Sudamericana.

Roland, A. (1996). *Cultural Pluralism and Psychoanalysis*. New York: Routledge.

Sabatini Scalmati, A. (2000). Memorie congelate memorie evitate: a proposito della relazione terapeutica con le vittime di tortura. In: *Richard e Piggle*, 2.

Sandler, J. (1987). The background of safety. In: *From Safety to Superego*. London: Karnac.

Sironi, F. (1992). Une pratique sous influence. *Nouvelle Revue d'Ethnopsychiatrie*, 22/23: 19–30.

Slavica, J. & Ivan, U. (2001). Linking objects in the process of mourning for sons disappeared in war. *Croatian Medical Journal*, 43(2): 234–239, 2002.

Smith, C. (2001). *Proud of Me. Speaking out against Sexual Violence and HIV*. Sea Point, South Africa: Penguin.

Sohn-Rettel, A. (1978). *Intellectual and Manual Labour, a Critique of Scientific Epistemology*. Atlantic Highlands, NJ: Humanities Press.

Srinath, S. (1998). Identificatory processes in trauma. In: C. Garland (Ed.), *Understanding Trauma: A Psychoanalytic Approach* (pp. 139–151). London: Tavistock.

Sturluson, S. (1225). *Heimskringla or The History of the Kings of Norway*. L. M. Hollander (Trans.). Austin, TX: University of Texas Press, 1964.

Sucharov, M. (2001). The infinite, the sacred and contextualism. Paper presented at the 24th *Annual International Conference on the Psychology of the Self*, San Francisco.

Sutton, A. (1991). Deprivation entangled and disentangled. *Journal of Child Psychotherapy*, 17(1): 61–77.

Terr, L. C. (1991). Childhood traumas: An outline and overview. *American Journal of Psychiatry*, 148(1): 10–20.

Tisseron, S. (1992). *La honte. Psychanalyse d'un lien social*. Paris: Dunod.

Trentini, B. (n. d.) Miroir, mon beau miroir. Musée Critique de la Sorbonne (MUCRI), Le Caravage: Tête de Méduse. http://mucri.univ-paris1.fr/mucri11/article.php3?id_article=118 (accessed July 4, 2011).

Van der Veer, G. (1993). Psychotherapy with young adult political refugees. A developmental approach. In: J. P. Wilson & B. Raphael (Eds.), *International Handbook of Traumatic Stress Syndromes* (pp. 651–657). New York: Plenum Press.

Vernant, J.-P. & Detienne, M. (1974). *Les ruses de l'intelligence: La métis des Grecs*. Paris: Flammarion.

Vidal-Naquet, P. (1994). Preface to Simon Doubnov's *Histoire moderne du peuple juif*, translated from the Russian by Samuel Jankélévitch. Paris: Le Cerf.

Viñar, M. (1988). Violencia social y realidad en psicoanálisis. In: J. Puget & R. Kaës (Eds.), *Violencia de Estado y Psicoanálisis*. Buenos Aires: Editorial Lumen, 2006.

Waintrater, R. (1999). Ouvrir les images: Les dangers du témoignage. In: *Le risque de l'étranger: Soin psychique et politique*. Paris: Dunod (Collection Inconscient et Culture).

Waintrater, R. (2004). Le pacte testimonial. In: *Témoignage et trauma—implications psychanalytiques* (pp. 65–97). Paris: Dunod.

Waisbrot, D., et al. (2003). *Clinica psicoanalítica ante la catástrofe social la experiencia Argentina*. Buenos Aires: Ed. Paidos.

Wardi, D. (1993). *Le candele della memoria*. Milan: Sansoni.

White, M. (1998). *Re-Authoring Lives: Interviews and Essays*. Adelaide, Australia: Dulwich.

Wieviorka, A. (1998). *L'ère du témoin*. Paris: Plon.

Winnicott, D. W. (1953). Transitional objects and transitional phenomena. In: *Playing and Reality* (pp. 1–25). London: Routledge, 1971.

Winnicott, D. W. (1967). The location of the cultural experience. In: *Playing and Reality* (pp. 95–103). London: Routledge, 1971.

Winnicott, D. W. (1974). Fear of breakdown. *International Journal of Psychoanalysis, 1*: 103–107.

Winnicott, D. W. (1990). *The Maturational Processes and the Facilitating Environment. Studies in the Theory of Emotional Development*. London: Karnac and Institute of Psychoanalysis.

Woodward, J. (1987). *The Lone Twin—Understanding Bereavement and Loss*. London: Free Association.

Young, L. & Gibb, E. (1998). Trauma and grievance. In: C. Garland (Ed.), *Understanding Trauma: A Psychoanalytic Approach* (pp. 81–95). London: Tavistock.

INDEX

For Product Safety Concerns and Information please contact our EU
representative GPSR@taylorandfrancis.com
Taylor & Francis Verlag GmbH, Kaufingerstraße 24, 80331 München, Germany

www.ingramcontent.com/pod-product-compliance
Lightning Source LLC
Chambersburg PA
CBHW070425270326
41926CB00014B/2942

9 7 8 1 8 5 5 7 5 7 9 6 7